NAPOLEON

Napoleon

Roger Dufraisse

Translation and Introduction by
Steven Englund

McGraw-Hill, Inc.
New York   St. Louis   San Francisco   Auckland   Bogotá
Caracas   Lisbon   London   Madrid   Mexico   Milan   Montreal   New Delhi
Paris   San Juan   Singapore   Sydney   Tokyo   Toronto

Napoleon

Copyright © 1992 by McGraw-Hill, Inc. All rights reserved.
Copyright © 1990 by Lyceum Books, Inc. All rights reserved.
Copyright © 1987 by Presses Universitaires de France. All
rights reserved. Printed in the United States of America.
Except as permitted under the United States Copyright Act of
1976, no part of this publication may be reproduced or
distributed in any form or by any means, or stored in a data
base or retrieval system, without the prior written permission
of the publisher.

1 2 3 4 5 6 7 8 9 0 DOH DOH 9 0 9 8 7 6 5 4 3 2 1

ISBN 0-07-018045-8

The editor was David Follmer;
the production supervisor was Kathryn Porzio.
R. R. Donnelley & Sons Company was printer and binder.

Library of Congress Cataloging-in Publication Data
Dufraisse, Roger.
　　[Napoléon. English]
　　Napoleon / Roger Dufraisse: translation and introduction
by Steven Englund.
　　　p.　　cm.
Translation of: Napoléon.
Includes bibliographical references.
ISBN 0-07-018045-8
　　1. Napoleon I, Emperor of the French, 1769-1821.
2. France–Kings and rulers–Biography.　　3. France– History–
Revolution, 1789-1799.　　4. France–History–Consulate and
Empire–1799-1815.　　5. Europe– History–1789-1815.
6. France–History, Military–1789-1815.
I. Title.
DC203D7913　　1992
944.05'092–dc20
[B]　　　　　　　　　　　　　　　　　　　　　90-6169

CONTENTS

Translator's Introduction

*W*hat, another book on Napoleon? Do specialists of the First French Empire ever get inured to the reproach implicit in that exclamation? One longs to reply, "Ah, and if only you knew the half of it. Why, there are actually more published sources on Napoleon than there are days since he died—as of 5 May 1990, the 169th anniversary of his death, there will be 61,685 volumes" ("of which I haven't read 5 percent," the more honest scholar will add).

So, why another? Certainly one must not overlook the now-familiar mentions of the singular contributions of Napoleon I as general and statesman, or the well-known antinomies about the emperor as incarnation of the Revolution yet restorer of the church, and so on. One can point to the endurance of the Napleonic legend in France or discourse on the impact of the Civil Code on Louisiana. But, frankly, any student of Napoleon worth his salt knows that these truisms are not what sustain the world's interest in this man.

Old questions are sometimes best resolved with old answers. The great American journalist of the 1920s, William Bolitho, expressed with incomparable succinctness why we are fascinated by Bonaparte: "Thousands of little

Italian boys to the present day wish to be kings, and their brothers to be dukes. No one has ever pulled the picture towards them, sucked this destiny out of the universe with the same titanic intensity of want, the same centripetal longing, as Napoleon."

Napoleon's "destiny never ceases to provoke men's reflection and stimulate their imagination," writes Roger Dufraisse in the brief book that follows, and, he adds, the story will "never be finished, never completely written." He is right. Few subjects are so evergreen as the "little Corsican" who made himself a general at twenty-six, dictator of France at thirty, and ruler of most of Western Europe at thirty-five. Alexander and Caesar spring to mind, but they started out with more than Napoleon, they accomplished less, and in all events we know comparatively little about them, so that they stir our imagination less forcefully.

Setting books aside for a moment, consider just some of the attention Napoleon has received in the world of entertainment in recent times: a Broadway play, a long-running Paris musical, and a television miniseries—not to mention the biggest hit of all: the hugely successful revival of the shamelessly romantic (and romanticized) film *Napoleon*, made in 1926 by Abel Gance. It comes as no surprise that the first French emperor has absorbed more celluloid than Lincoln, Lenin, and Joan of Arc combined.

Yet the miles of film exposed cannot compare with the tons of paper consumed by Napoleon. The humming machine that is First Empire studies continues to turn out books and articles at an astounding rate—hundreds each year, in many languages. Recently we've seen the appearance of two fine large dictionaries of Napoleon and Napoleana, as well as a 280-page book devoted merely to listing and annotating Napoleonic studies since 1945 (see the bibliography).

Nor is the secondary literature the only theater of operations where a Napoleon specialist must field an army. It may even be the lesser front compared to keeping abreast of the primary sources—state documents, newspapers, letters, memoirs, and the like—that are published or discovered or newly utilized from time to time. In sum, we do not demur when Roger Dufraisse notes that Napoleon's hold on our imagination is even more secure than was his hold on France or Europe, which, by the fleeting standards of world conquest, was fairly secure.

And yet, at the risk of sounding perverse, one must concur with a number of leading scholars of the First Empire who for some time now have pointed out that despite all this industriousness, we do not really have an up-to-date, *complete* biography of Napoleon in English. There have been a number of overviews of recent vintage—notably Jean Tulard's *Napoleon, the Myth of the Saviour* (originally published in 1974), though unhappily it is available in such a poor English translation that it is untrustworthy. Yet we do not have a full-length synthetic biography of Napoleon that *both* takes into account the new research and documentation that have appeared in the last generation, and does literary justice to the sheer size and ungovernability of so legendary and complex a subject.

One reason we do not may be that nobody feels moved enough to write such a biography. Consider the classic writers on Napoleon of yesteryear—formidable pens such as Chateaubriand, de Staël, Stendhal, Thiers, Taine, and Tolstoy, and, in our own century, the German novelist Emil Ludwig. Or think of the great academicians and university historians, such as Sorel, Pariset, Seignobos, and Bainville. They were one and all fierce partisans who labored years to produce magnificent attacks on, or apologies for, Napoleon. The key to their appeal, and to their motivation, may well be, in the last analysis, precisely the triumph of their engagement over their detachment.

Turning to the writers and historians of today, however, one has the contrary impression that although the *Sitzfleisch** may be ample, the high emotion that fueled those classic "life and times" biographies is perhaps lacking. For a number of years now scholars of the French Revolution have been moving away from strong "pro" and "con" general takes on the Revolution. The same phenomenon is occurring in First Empire studies, to the point that nowadays a historiographer would have a hard time making exciting reading out of the relatively slight and nuanced differences of opinion among, say, Tulard, Connelly, Bergeron, or Dufraisse in their overall view of Napoleon.

Let us take for example the very useful compilation of selected interpretations of *Napoleon and His Times* that Professors Frank Kafker and James Laux have recently assembled. If we compare it to Pieter Geyl's 1944 study, *Napoleon: For and Against,* we are instantly struck by the profoundly smaller range and violence of viewpoint on the emperor himself. Pitched battles over character and motivation have become irritable skirmishes over more purely historical questions, such as the impact on England of the continental system (and blockade), or the role of nationalism in the Spanish uprising of 1809–1812. The useful work that fol-

---

Sitzfleisch—a German term denoting the *gluteus maximus* and connoting the ability to sit still for a long time, as in the act of doing research.

lows is, as it happens, both characteristic of the more recent approach and timely. The Dufraisse *Napoléon* first appeared in 1987 as a title in the well-known *Que Sais-Je?* [What Do I Know?] collection of the *Presses Universitaires de France*— a series designed to provide general readers with brief but state-of-the-question overviews of even the most complex topics. As one of France's most respected practitioners of First Empire studies (specializing in social and economic history), Roger Dufraisse was a logical candidate to write the new *Que Sais-Je?* volume on Napoleon. He is director of studies at the acclaimed School of Advanced Study [*Ecole Pratique des Hautes Etudes*, 4th Section].

One has only to compare Dufraisse's take on Napoleon with that of his esteemed predecessor in the same series— Henri Calvet, in 1953—to see that Dufraisse's book constitutes a fine example of the path that current scholarly writing about Napoleon has taken. Whereas Calvet produced a genuine life story (perforce brief, to suit the genre), Dufraisse leans more toward history than biography, that is, more toward the record of collectivities (nations, classes, governments, institutions, and the like) than toward an attempt to give coherence to the life of an individual.

Now admittedly in the case of a Napoleon Bonaparte, it is dangerous to draw overly neat distinctions between the story of a life and that of an era. More than any other in the annals of modern Europe, Napoleon's biography coincided with, and profoundly affected, the history of his times. Germaine de Staël, possibly the greatest literary talent among Napoleon's (often admiring) enemies, wrote of him, "It was the first time since the Revolution that one person's name was on everyone's lips. Until [Napoleon], it was said: 'The Constituent Assembly has done such-and-

such, or the people, or the Convention.' Now the talk was
all about this man who was going to put himself in the
place of all others, and render the human race anonymous
by monopolizing celebrity for himself." A latter-day biographer of Napoleon, Sir Herbert Butterfield, said it more
succinctly: "We are spectators now of the great unrolling,
and it is no longer biography—it is the whole history of
Europe that is in question."

Disclaimers in place, however, it remains no less true
that Professor Dufraisse characterizes the tendency of our
age by focusing more on the times than on the man. Thus,
he has well-developed views on such historical questions
as popular reaction to military conscription—he sees it as
less hostile and political than is usually thought; or the war
of Spanish liberation—which he, unlike some recent scholars, finds "retrograde" in its social make-up and political
motivation. Again, Dufraisse is fascinated by the consequences of the continental system and blockade, to which
he pays far closer attention proportionally than most historians, and whose long-term effects he possibly overesti-
mates.

In short, Dufraisse definitely has viewpoints and even
biases. (The perceptive student may, for example, spot a
certain Gallic archness, if not outright hostility, toward England in the author's attitude.) But they are not much concerned with Napoleon, himself, on whom Dufraisse has no
strong or original view. The Napoleon who emerges in these
pages is a man of extraordinary gifts who, as he attains
extraordinary success and supreme power, gradually loses
control of his own emotions and drives. He is the Jacobin
son of the Revolution who betrays (most of) the revolutionary heritage in France while simultaneously serving it

abroad, especially if it paid to do so. Beyond this familiar view, the author has no interest either in "yanking out [Napoleon's] coattails and setting fire to them" (to quote Bernard DeVoto) nor, still less, in pursuing what another biographer terms "The Guildenstern instinct" (referring to Hamlet's reproach to Guildenstern, "You would pluck out the heart of my mystery").

Professor Harold Parker, one of the grand old men of American Napoleonic studies, recently called for a serious, full-length "interpretive psychosocial biography that [would] integrate Napoleon's personality and life with the Corsican and French societies through which he moved." Until such time as someone feels called upon to move that particular mountain, Monsieur Dufraisse's fine, short survey will serve us well indeed.

Steven Englund
Waupaca, Wisconsin, and
Paris, France

Preface

*F*irst Consul at thirty, emperor at thirty-five, prisoner at Saint Helena at forty-six, Napoleon reigned as monarch for only ten years. When he was forced from the center of public life, the empire he founded and the system by which he had dominated half of Europe collapsed. And yet, as Jean Tulard writes: "The Napoleonic adventure stands as much at the origin of Egypt's take-off as of Latin America's independence; it precipitated England's seizure of Australia and it provided Java with a system of trade routes that has not changed since. The wars it gave rise to had their echo from the Great Lakes to the shores of the Indian Ocean. One of the first historians of Napoleon was a Chinese, succeeded only a short time later by a Brazilian. In short, a universal impact."

Right down to our own day, Napoleon's tomb in Les Invalides is invariably the monument that receives the largest number of visitors to Paris, the majority of them foreign. In Paris, a musical entitled *Napoleon* ran for several years (it closed in 1986). More than 170 years after his death, Napoleon still fascinates, interests, and irritates, as his destiny never ceases to provoke people's reflection and stimulate their imagination.

In 1953, the *Que Sais-Je?* Collection was enriched by Henri Calvet's magisterial *Napoléon*, which the present volume cold not hope to replace. One would even err in reproaching Calvet for his Franco-centrism, for if it is true that Napoleon was King of Italy, Mediator of the Helvetic Confederation, and Protector of the Confederation of the Rhine, and if it is true that his actions exercised an influence that spilled over the boundaries of old Europe, this man was still, first and foremost, First Consul of the French Republic, then Emperor of the French (notwithstanding that his scepter also held sway over Italians, Germans, Belgians, Dutch, Swiss, and Catalans).

This book attempts to present the historical research done on Napoleon and his time during the past thirty-five years. But if it does not claim to be exhaustive or definitive, this is perhaps because the story of Napoleon "will never be finished, never completely written."

CHAPTER 1

Napoleon Bonaparte
Before Brumaire

W hen, at the height of his power, Napoleon declared that he felt himself as much the heir of Saint Louis as of the Committee of Public Safety, he clearly meant that he accepted the entire heritage of the history of France, but it was perhaps also his way of recognizing that the Old Regime and the Revolution were, one and another, the twin sources of his prodigious career.

1. From Corsica to Command of the Army of Italy

Napoleone Buonaparte—thus he signed himself until 1795— was indeed born French, for he came into the world on 15 August 1769 in Ajaccio, the capital of an island that only fifteen months before had been acquired by France. His family had fought at Paoli's side in the resistance to the annexation, but they ended by rallying to the French after a few months. Not until 1793, after the defeat of all the grand plans by which he had hoped to put his family at the center of the island's political life, would Napoleon fi-

1

nally cease to feel himself Corsican and consider himself
French.

His Family

Though not living in opulence, the Buonaparte family was
not poor. Twelve children, of whom eight survived, were
born to the minor provincial nobleman Charles Buonaparte
and his wife, Maria Laetizia Ramolino. In order of birth,
Napoleone was the fourth, the second surviving child.

To feed such a numerous family, the father, after rallying to the French party, never relented in his efforts to
solicit a job and favors from the new governor, Marbeuf.
Finally, in 1779, he was named deputy for the nobility of
Corsica at the court of Louis XVI, and left for the continent,
accompanied by his two eldest sons—Joseph, destined for
an ecclesiastical career, and Napoleone. Both boys were admitted to the school of Autun, but the younger remained
only two months. On 15 May 1779, thanks to a scholarship
from the king, Napoleone entered the military school of
Brienne.

School Years

Brienne, run by the Minimist fathers, was one of twelve
such military schools created by the war minister, Saint-
Germain. At the king's expense, 650 noble sons acquired
the traditional profession of arms. After two years there,
the best of students were admitted to the school in Paris.
Thus, the French monarchy's solicitude for the minor nobility permitted Buonaparte to embrace a military career.

Puny in appearance, lonely for his family, expressing
himself in poor French, victimized by his schoolmates' teas-
ing, Napoleone lived through painful days at Brienne. Many

years later, however, looking back on his school days, he claimed that he harbored a positive memory of Brienne. He would make Bourrienne, one of his friends from school, a personal secretary, later Councillor of State, and finally French charge d'affaires at Hamburg. Another classmate, Bourgeois de Joussaint, became Prefect of the Marne, while Breton, Napoleone's principal at Brienne, was appointed headmaster of the *lycée* of Reims. On the other hand, he did no favors—quite the contrary—for Pichegru, his former mathematics assistant instructor.

Buonaparte was a mediocre student at Brienne. He had to apply himself to the study of the Latin authors—Cicero, Titus Livy, Horace, Virgil. But he devoured the *Lives* of Plutarch, the great authors of the French classical theater, and the *Funeral Orations* of Bossuet. He was passionately interested in history and geography. His preferences ran toward "the most virtuous men of humanity," notably Caesar, in his eyes the highest model of human greatness, at once a man of war, a statesman, and a writer. The young Napoleone wished to emulate Caesar by "collecting professions." Successful in his first attempt at graduation examinations, Buonaparte left Brienne with the title of gentleman-cadet and on 19 March 1784 entered the Paris military school of the Champ-de-Mars. Here all his teachers, including the great mathematician Monge, who taught artillery, declared themselves satisfied with his work. Indeed, Buonaparte's formidable command of mathematics obtained for him the brevet of a lieutenant of artillery after a single year of study, although ordinarily two were required. At the time he was sixteen years old and two weeks (September 1785).

"I am more a citizen of military school than of Corsica, for, since the age of nine, I was a student at Brienne [and later at the Champs-de-Mars]," he would say at Saint Helena, a claim not entirely consistent with the facts, for until 1793, Buonaparte continued to think of himself as Corsican and to nourish a blind hostility against French domination, which he still hoped to see his countrymen reject.

Earliest Assignments

On leaving the Ecole du Champ-de-Mars, second lieutenant Napoleone Buonaparte was assigned to the Regiment de la Fère of the Royal Corps of Artillery, stationed in Valence. Now began the monotonous, vexing life of provincial garrison duty. The young officer showed little devotion to such service: from 28 October 1785 to 30 September 1791, he took thirty-eight months of leave, compared to only thirty-three months of duty in such places as Valence, Lyon, Douai, Auxonne, and Valence again. He lived impecuniously on his modest salary and spent most of his days of leave with his family in Ajaccio. After his father died (February 1785), Napoleone gradually replaced his eldest brother, Joseph, as the head of the family.

The school years and the years when he was a fantôme officer were nonetheless decisive for his military training. Gribeauval had not been content merely to supply French artillery with excellent new materiel (1765), he had also established a demanding new training program for officers. Thus Buonaparte had to learn all the infantry manoeuvres as well as study all the circumstances in which artillery could be used. Through the lectures he attended at Paris and Auxonne, supplemented by exercises with maps and in the field, Buonaparte acquired his first notions of general tactics. At Auxonne he had as an instructor the chevalier du Teil, brother of the author of *The Use of the New Artillery*, a book that elaborated a doctrine that exploited the power and mobility of the new ordnance.

Buonaparte completed his field training by studying the French campaign in Italy during 1745 and 1746 and the campaigns of Frederick the Great during the Seven Years War. In addition, he attentively read Feuquière's *Memoirs of the War* and especially Guibert's *General Essay on Tactics* (1773), which defended the idea that, above all else, manoeuvres had to be undertaken swiftly but in magnitude, with divisional units containing all arms (cavalry and artillery as well as infantry). These ideas required reducing the size of most units and services, flexible formations, and decentralizing command—all reforms that either Napoleone himself or Carnot would effect. Guibert, finally, had little respect for immobile, fortified defenses, and on this point, Napoleone, though not usually the slave of his readings, would be perhaps too loyal to the master's doctrine. Overconfident about his talent for manoeuvre, he would neglect fortifications in the interior, an error that would prove fatal in 1814.

Because of the heavy reading regimen of his school years and, even more, of his years of garrison duty, Napoleone must have turned himself into, if not exactly a man of culture, then at least a man of great knowledge. He was as acquainted with the *Digests* of Justinian (entire pages of which, when the Code Napoleon was being drafted, he could recite instantly from memory) as with the writings of Rousseau and Raynal (both partisans of an independent Corsica), of Voltaire, of Rollin (the reigning master of Roman history) of Mirabeau, and of Necker.

During these years, Buonaparte did some writing of his own that not only reveals his unbounded admiration for the Corsican patriot Paoli, but generally shows that its author, like so many artillery officers, had been won over to new ideas. Thus, one can read in his *Dissertation on Royal Authority* (October 1788): "There are few kings who would not have deserved to be overthrown."

While he was at Auxonne, Napoleone witnessed the earliest disorders of the Revolution. In April 1789, at Seurre, he and his company participated in a military operation to preserve order, during which he uttered revealing words about his own outlook: "You decent people (*honnêtes gens*), go home. I shall open fire only on the rabble." In July, after returning to Auxonne, he watched the crowd invade the local tax office and burn official records. In August, his regiment mutinied, leading Napoleone to believe that the collapse of royal authority would finally permit the realization of his dream of Corsican independence. He took an immediate leave from the army and in September of 1789 was once again in Ajaccio.

The Revolution: Buonaparte Becomes Bonaparte

Having scarcely returned home, Napoleone met his first disappointment: the Revolution here had succeeded only in reviving the ancient feuds among local clans. Paoli, while adhering to the principles of 1789, thought of the French as only half-brothers [*confrères*]; he remained a Corsican patriot. He therefore accepted with repugnance the offers of help from the pro-French sons of his old enemy, Charles Buonaparte, who nevertheless threw themselves with abandon into the political battles, declaimed at the clubs, and wrote pamphlets and speeches.

In February 1791, Buonaparte finally returned to his garrison at Auxonne, where he was named first lieutenant and joined the local Jacobin club. He competed for a literary prize of the Lyon Academy with an essay on the subject, "Which Truths and Which Feelings Are the Most Important to Inculcate into Men for Their Own Happiness?" It amounted to forty pages of banalities, combining side by side an unreserved approbation of the ideas of Rousseau and Raynal, a no less fulsome condemnation of despotism, and yet one more uncritical encomium of the reforms that Paoli had accomplished in Corsica. The judges had the good sense not to award him a prize. In another essay, inspired by the attempted flight of the king, Buonaparte showed himself a partisan, in France at least, of republicanism, an idea whose time was about to arrive.

Although war threatened French frontiers, Lieutenant Buonaparte nevertheless took another leave to return to Corsica (September 1791). Because he was absent from the general inspection of his regiment on 1 January 1792, his name was cut from the roster of the army. However, this permitted him to be legally elected lieutenant-colonel of a battalion of volunteers, organized in Corsica, as in all the other departments of France. In this office, on 9 April he opened fire in the streets of Ajaccio on the lower-class protesters against the Civil Constitution of the Clergy, winning for himself the hostility of the counterrevolutionary party led by Pozzo di Borgo. Then, against the orders of his colonel, he took the Ajaccio citidel. Later, at Paoli's direct order, he was forced to turn it over to the regular army.

Now, seeking to protect himself should he fail in Corsica, Napoleone decided to return to Paris to reinstate himself in the French army. On 20 June 1792, he witnessed the invasion of the Tuileries, an event that confirmed more deeply his belief that society comprised two camps: the "populace" and the decent people. His sympathies lay entirely with the (wealthier) decent people, and especially with their current leader, the Marquis de La Fayette. As long as Napoleone remained in public life, his hostility to the "rabble" never deserted him.

On 10 July 1792, a decree signed by Louis XVI recommissioned him in the army. The invasion of the Tuileries on 10 August and the fall of the monarchy offered a new occasion for Napoleone to betray his contempt for a king who had capitulated under duress to the populace. Instead of leaving with his regiment for the war at the French frontier, he preferred to return to Corsica and reclaim his old rank of lieutenant-colonel in the battalion of volunteers.

After the king of Sardinia declared war on France, Buonaparte and his unit were ordered to occupy the small Sardinian-held islets of the Maddalena, but the operation failed (23 February 1793). Soon after, Paoli broke with France and, possibly because of accusations raised against him by Lucien Buonaparte in the Jacobin Club of Toulon, was arrested as a traitor and an agent of England. The town of Ajaccio broke out in insurrection; the Buonapartes faced an alliance of the royalist forces of Pozzo di Borgo as well as the Corsican patriots grouped behind Paoli. Their family home was sacked; Laetizia and the younger children fled to Calvi, then by ship to Toulon (11 June 1793), then to Marseille. Thereafter, Napoleone and his family sided firmly with France, less in sympathy for the Revolution than out of rejection by a Corsican regime temporarily controlled by Paoli.

At least until 1815, Corsica would strongly resent the Buonapartes. The results of the plebiscites of the Years VIII, X, and XII were less successful there than elsewhere, just as the proportion of draft-resisters and deserters under the Consulat and Empire was highest there.

Napoleone Buonaparte had been wise not to quit the French army irrevocably. After leaving Corsica for good, he assumed command of a company in his old regiment, now stationed at Nice. For a short time later he was stationed in Avignon, in the service of convoys in the French Army of Italy. At this time, Provence blazed in full federalist insurrection against Paris and the Revolution. This furnished him with the theme for a work of fiction, *Supper at Beaucaire*, a well-informed political piece that criticized federalism and adhered to Jacobin thought, while nevertheless adopting a generally conciliationist attitude that the writer would try to use to good advantage after Brumaire.

On 16 September 1793, "Citizen Buonaparte, a well-read captain who was preparing to leave for Italy with the army," was reassigned to other duty by two Representatives on Mission, Salicetti and Gasparin. He was given command of the artillery of the army of siege at Toulon, a city that had been turned over to the English by federalist rebels.

Napoleone had strained relations with Carteaux, the former housepainter become general, who commanded the besiegers. Against his superior's wishes, and considering the topography of the site, Buonaparte thought he could take the city with cannon supported by infantry. He managed to obtain from the Committee of Public Safety not only reinforcements for the artillery but also its subordination to a different commander, General du Teil, Napoleone's former instructor from Brienne. Du Teil promptly gave him carte blanche. Even better, with Salicetti's help, Buonaparte managed to have Dugommier, who accepted his plans for the reduction of Toulon, replace Carteaux. After a vigorous bombardment, which forced the Anglo-Spanish fleet into the open sea, the city was taken (17–19 December 1793).

On 22 December, after Augustin Robespierre, the younger brother of Maximilien, proposed him, Buonaparte was made a brigadier general. His new rank gave him the opportunity to denounce to the Committee of Public Safety the enormous waste in military administration, in particular in the departments of materiel and personnel. On 24 March 1794, thanks again to the younger Robespierre, Napoleone took command of the artillery in the Army of Italy, now stationed on the frontier. He conceived the idea (brilliantly acted on two years later) that the key to defeating Austria lay in taking Italy, but could not yet convince Carnot.

On 9 Thermidor (27 July 1794), Robespierre fell, as did Augustin, who had asked to share his brother's fate. Thereafter all "Robespierrists" felt threatened. Trying to clear themselves of suspicion, Salicetti and two of his colleagues signed (8 August 1794) a decree for the arrest of Buonaparte, whom they accused of plotting to "destroy liberty." On 11 August he was incarcerated in the fort at Antibes, but because no plausible charge could be sustained against him, he was freed on the 20th. Ten days later his rank was restored, but not his command.

On 29 March 1795, Napoleone learned that he had been named general of artillery in the Army of the West, which had been assigned to put an end to the Chouan rebellion. But he had no desire to take a post that would so distance him from the Army of Italy, nor, for that matter, from Désirée Clary, daughter of a Marseille merchant, to whom he was engaged.

On 28 May Napoleone went to Paris and had a falling out at the Committee of Public Safety with Aubry, who was in charge of all promotions and transferrals of general officers, and who was hostile to former Jacobins. The young artillery general found himself shifted to infantry, a demotion. In retaliation, Buonaparte inundated the committee with a thousand different projects. To get rid of him, the committee attached him to the bureau of topography, where he not only considerably deepened his knowledge of military science, but also attracted the attention of Carnot.

Studying the fine collection of maps and plans kept in the War Office, Buonaparte reconfirmed his belief that in war it is best to focus on the concrete. The moment he became his own master, he created his own bureau of topography, which he outfitted with the finest collection of maps, plans, and statistical documents, all kept rigorously up to date. On 30 August 1795, he requested that the committee authorize him to go to Turkey, where the sultan was seeking foreign officers to help him modernize his army. But his request was denied and on 30 September he was cut from the list of active general officers for refusing his posting to the Army of the West.

At half pay, living in straitened circumstances, Buonaparte now saw his plan to marry Désirée Clary floundering. Based on intimate experience, he wrote a novel, *Clisson and Eugénie*. He also proved indefatigable in courting the Committee of Public Safety, whose offices he haunted. There he met Barras, former Representative to the Army of Italy. The personification of a certain kind of corrupt nobleman who played a large role in the Revolution, Barras had scandalously enriched himself while "serving" the state. Thermidor brought him to the foreground, and he would now do the same for Buonaparte.

The repentant regicides and terrorists known as the Thermidorians wished to secure their hold on power. Therefore, in drafting the Constitution of the Year III they founded a directorial regime that they hoped would forever close the door to royalists, to moderates who had voted against executing Louis XVI, and, of course, to Jacobins. On the eve of its dissolution, the Convention, to avoid a probable royalist victory in the coming elections, voted that two-thirds of the future members of the bicameral legislature of the new regime must be drawn from its own body. Exasperated, the royalists resolved to raise an insurrection against the Convention in the wealthy neighborhoods of Paris. Since Thermidor, and more especially, since 12 Germinal and 1 Prairial (1 April and 20 May 1795), the Convention found it could no longer count on the support of the Parisian sansculottes. This was largely its own fault; to checkmate the people during Prairial, the Convention had had to turn loose the army, now its only defense against attacks from the left or the right, the street, or the ballot box. On 5 October 1795, to parry the royalist thrust, it handed over to Barras command of Army of the Interior.

Holding no illusions about his own military talents, Barras had reassigned to the Army of the Interior several generals looking for work, including Buonaparte. The latter saved the Convention on 13 Vendémiaire, Year IV (5 October 1795). Considering the terrain, it seems certain that Napoleone did not (contrary to legend) fire grapeshot at the "collets noirs" (aristocrats in black lace collars) before the church of Saint-Roch. If he completely crushed the royalists, it was because Murat successfully captured the greatly needed cannon of Sablons, and because Buonaparte knew how to manoeuver the Convention's troops to clear out the Tuileries, the Louvre, and the Palais-Royal.

On 26 October, Buonaparte replaced Barras as commander in chief of the Army of the Interior. "General Vendémiaire," as he was now called, had won a solid reputation for republicanism. Hereafter the forces promoting the Revolution against the royalist threat considered him as one of their own. To prove how completely French he had become, the general from now on signed himself Bonaparte.

During this period, he married Josephine de Beauharnais, a "merry widow" seven years his senior, whose aristocratic husband had embraced the Revolution only to be forced to climb the scaffold. Napoleon had met her through Barras at a soirée at his home before 13 Vendémiaire and had fallen suddenly and violently in love. His victory in the streets had made him the man of the moment and also taken care of his financial needs. He knew no peace until he had convinced her to legalize their relationship by marriage. The ceremony took place on 9 March 1795. Because of his genuine love for Josephine (he was, it should be recalled, an admirer of Goethe's romantic *Sorrows of Young Werther*) Napoleon long tolerated his wife's indifference and infidelities. Married for love, thirteen years later she was repudiated for reasons of state.

2. Bonaparte in Italy (1796–1797)

In twenty months of campaigning, Bonaparte revealed his military genius to an astonished Europe. He also made peace on the Continent after years of war and acquired the political, diplomatic, and administrative experience of a statesman. On 2 March 1796, Carnot, after reading Bonaparte's plans for the campaign, named him commander in chief of the Army of Italy. He was not yet twenty-seven years old. The government had thought that Austria must be defeated in Germany, using the large armies of Jourdan and Moreau, while the Army of Italy would create a diversion, dominate the Italian princes, and remove any threat from the Alpine frontier.

Arriving at Nice on 23 March 1796, Napoleon immediately took in hand a starving, poorly disciplined army accustomed to pillage: 35,000 foot soldiers, 4,000 cavalry, and a deficient artillery corps. But the soldiery was of high quality; most of the infantry had fought in three previous campaigns. Most divisional generals—Augereau, Masséna, Sérurier, and La Harpe—were excellent, if patently untrustworthy and ambitious.

Bonaparte struck with the speed of lightning. In ten days, by victories at Montenotte (12 April 1796), Milesimo (13 April), Dego (14 April), and Mondavi (21 April), he separated the Austrians from their Piedmontese allies. The latter, isolated, readily signed the armistice of Cherasco (28 April), because King Victor-Amadeus feared that the French army would promote a Jacobin revolution in his realm.

By signing the armistice, Bonaparte overstepped the law, for only commissioners, in this instance, Garreau and Salicetti, had this authority. In addition, he ignored the Directory's intention to republicanize Italy. On the other hand, the government could only approve his actions. Beset at home by Babouvists, the Directory could hardly support Jacobins in Piedmont. In any case, the money pouring in from the newly conquered lands made the pill easier for the Directors to swallow. The peace, signed in Paris on 3 June, corresponded to the wishes of the Directory: recognition of the annexation of Savoy and Nice, and a war indemnity of 3 million francs. With war indemnities so plentiful, Bonaparte decided to pay his army half its wages in coin. This decision (normally made by governments, not generals) turned the Army of Italy into the army of Bonaparte.

On 5 May, the Army of Italy undertook the conquest of Lombardy, defended by a 35,000-man army of Austrians under the command of Beaulieu. The Austrians, bivouacked on the left bank of the Po, behind Tessin, fell prey to Bonaparte's rapid movement to the south (which violated Parma's neturality) and crossed the river at Plaisance. Bonaparte threw the enemy back to the Adda, to the bridge of Lodi (10 May), and on 16 May he entered Milan, where he was greeted as a liberator by the Patriot party, which had taken power three days before. The Austrians had escaped encirclement only by violating the neutrality of Venice. Thus they established themselves strongly in Mantua, to which Bonaparte laid siege on 18 July. Previously, (19 May) the duke of Parma had signed an armistice with Bonaparte that cost him 20 million francs and twenty masterpiece paintings. Again the French general had acted in the place of the commissioners assigned to his army.

On 13 May 1796, however, Bonaparte had received a letter from Carnot ordering him not to invade the Tyrol from the south but to proceed into central Italy to garner more reparations, dethrone the pope, and, ultimately, push on to Naples. The general complied, but before doing so, he threw another 20-million-franc indemnity on the Milanese, and, acting on his own authority, accorded an armistice to the duke of Modena, who had to come up with 7½ million francs and twenty paintings.

The welcome given him by the Milanese had converted Bonaparte to the cause of an independent republic in the north of Italy, but the troubles that broke out in Lombardy behind his own lines, largely because of the crushing reparations (this time levied by Salicetti) revealed to Napoleon the strength of Italian national sentiment. Thereafter, he did all he could to restrain it, and, rather than create independent Italian states, he did not tolerate more than the setting up of vassal states of France.

Marching into central Italy, the army occupied Bologna, in the Papal States (20 June 1796). Bonaparte here showed himself shrewdly prudent, for he weighed the importance of religion. Knowing that he would return north, where the Austrian forces had been reinforced, he imposed, again by his own authority, an armistice on the pope (22 June) that obliged His Holiness to pay 15½ million francs in gold and silver, and to turn over materiel valued at 4½ million francs to the French army.

On 27 July, this time acting on the Directory's orders, he violated Tuscan neutrality in order to seize Livorno, where he destroyed all the English goods he found. Meanwhile, in the north, the Austrians under Wurmser had taken the offensive and were descending in three columns into the Tyrol, where they intended to raise the siege of Mantua. Lifting the siege before they arrived, Bonaparte, following Guibert's maxim (obtain with rapid manoeuver the equivalent of a numerical superiority at each site) struck with seriously outnumbered forces at each column separately and defeated each in turn, at Lonato (31 July), Castiglione

(5 August), and Bassano (8 September), Wurmser was forced to retreat to Mantua.

In Germany, meanwhile, the armies of Jourdan and Moreau had met with several serious defeats, so that the Army of Italy had become the Directory's single hope, and Bonaparte indispensable in their eyes. Knowing this and seeing the government's hesitation to dispatch him the reinforcements he was requesting, Bonaparte became even more stubborn. But getting his way was not always possible, even for Napoleon. The Directory, uninterested in the fate of the Duchy of Modena, permitted the deputies of Reggio, Ferrara, and Bologna, pushed by Bonaparte, to proclaim the Cispadane Republic (16 October 1796). This was the first of many states that Napoleon would create before 1810. He wanted the new Republic to strike on the political right against the partisans of the Old Regime, and on the left against the "anarchists," who were declared to be enemies of property. This was to be his own policy par excellence after 18 Brumaire. On the other hand, when the Directory prevented him from occupying and revolutionizing the Republic of Genoa, Napoleon had to content himself with forcing the Genovese to pay an indemnity of 4 million francs and close its ports to the British.

In November, 50,000 Austrians under the command of Alvinzi attacked the French from Friouli and the Tyrol in an attempt to lift the siege of Mantua. Hit hard on three sides, the French this time had to bend so as not to break. But after three days of furious fighting in the marshes of Arcola (15 to 17 November), they finally prevented the junction of the two Austrian armies.

Now both sides hardened their military positions. The Directory consented to send Bonaparte the 40,000 replacements he requested. Events were unfolding in France that doubtlessly would weigh heavily on Bonaparte's career. The preliminary talks with the English, opened in Lille and later moved to Paris, failed when the French refused to evacuate Belgium. It was clear from then on that the struggle between these two countries could end only with the complete defeat of one or the other. This war to the death with England was the most fearful legacy that the Revolution would leave Bonaparte. With the law of 10 Brumaire (31 October 1796), the Directory forbade all goods produced abroad, regardless of provenance, to enter French markets. The Directors wished to replace permanently British economic hegemony on the Continent with French. This was a major element in Napoleon's future continental system, and would prove to be one of the reasons for its failure.

In January 1797, the Austrians made their fourth attempt to free Mantua. With 50,000 men, Alvinzi struck at the French on three sides. The main force of Napoleon, concentrated on the plateau of Rivoli, recoiled under the shock of the attack, but Masséna arrived in time with his army and saved the situation (14 January 1797). The capitulation of Mantua on 2 February opened the road through the Tyrol.

The Directory now ordered Bonaparte to have done with the papacy and "extinguish the flame of religious fanaticism." He complied, while communicating to the cardinal-secretary of state that he would respect the pope and the Catholic Church. On 19 February 1797, Pius VI signed a peace at Tolentino that ceded the Comtat to the French, abandoned the Legations, and paid an additional 15 million francs in indemnities, together with many manuscripts, books, and works of art.

Meanwhile the Directory had reinstated its plans for the invasion of southern Germany and entrusted the task to two armies under the command of Hoche. Against the Army of Italy, now reinforced with 40,000 men, the Austrians opposed their best general, the Archduke Charles. For once enjoying numerical superiority, Bonaparte threw the mass of Charles's forces into disorder on the Tagliamento (16 March) and, marching through the eastern Alpine passes, swiftly took the offensive that led to Goritzia (21 March) and Klagenfurth (28 March).

Behind French lines, however, events were taking place that would serve Bonaparte's designs remarkably well. The Republic of Venice, which repulsed all offers of alliance with the French, instead became the victim of the French policy of "revolutionizing." Patriots in Bergamo and Brescia were encouraged by the French to rise up in insurrection, demanding that their governments join the Cisalpine Republic (11 to 18 March). But the crushing weight of the French occupation, the incessant republican propaganda, and the poorly disciplined French troops provoked the reverse effect. On the Monday following Easter (17 April), the inhabitants of Verona rose up, not against their own regime, but to massacre 400 French soldiers.

Meanwhile, the Army of the Sambre-and-Meuse had crossed the Rhine, and on 18 April 1797 Hoche was the victor at Neuwied. That same day, at Leoben, Bonaparte and the Austrian emissaries signed an armistice and preliminary peace treaty.

Bonaparte was eager to sign the peace, partly because he did not wish to share a triumph with his successful rival in Germany, and partly because the French elections of April 1797 saw the victory of the royalist and crypto-royalist partisans of a "small France" policy (one that favored the frontiers of 1789 augmented by only Nice, and Savoy). The Directory saw Italy as the bargaining chip to win the left bank of the Rhine and Belgium. At Leoben, Bonaparte offered the Austrians Dalmatia, Istria, and Venice in return for Belgium and Lombardy.

Such an operation, reminiscent of the partitions of Poland, stood directly in the tradition of the diplomacy of the Old Regime, and had already been imitated by the Convention and the Directory when they signed treaties with Prussia (1795) and Baden and Wurtemberg (1796) that wiped out in one sweep the old German ecclesiastical states of the right bank of the Rhine. The latter were given as compensation to those secular principalities of the left bank that had lost territory to France.

It remained to determine Venice's fate. On 2 May, France declared war in retribution for the "Veronese Easter" uprising. Venice fell on the 15th and sued for peace the next day. The doge's government had to pay the French 3 million francs in hard currency and an equivalent amount in supplies for the French navy, besides 5 warships, 20 paintings, and 500 manuscripts.

Formal peace negotiations with Austria opened at Udino on 29 May, though they did not stay Bonaparte's hand as he plunged ahead with the task of organizing his conquests. In Lombardy he founded a republic on the lines of the French. This was the Transpadane Republic, grouping together all the Lombard territories on the far side of the Po. Territories in the central part of the peninsula were united (9 July) into the Cisalpine Republic, made up of the Cispadane provices (Modena and the papal Legations) and the Venitian provinces of Bergamo and Brescia. He also incorporated into it the Valteline, whose inhabitants had let it be known that they wished to escape the tutelage of the Grisons. Bonaparte informed the Directory that the new state would have a constitution modeled on that of the Year III and that it would be linked to France by a route through the Simplon pass.

For Genoa, Bonaparte secretly favored the overthrow of the oligarchical regime and the proclamation of a Ligurian Republic, a republic whose independence he pretended to respect while actually exploiting it for all it was worth. In this treatment meted out to Italy, there was a true meeting of the minds, a rare instance, between Napoleon and the Directory.

But, for the rest, Bonaparte's policies greatly disturbed the French government, including the royalist majorities of the legislature. To win over the sympathy of those hostile to any return to the Old Regime, Bonaparte proposed to march with his troops against the Clichyans (moderate royalist constitutionalists). He furnished the Directory with proof of the treachery of General Pichegru, the president of the Council of Five Hundred, who had been "bought" by the royalists. The republican Directors then decided to divest the Directory of two of its moderates (royalists) and to purge the legislature of royalist deputies, even though the latter had been duly elected. In short, a coup d'etat was planned, and to execute it a republican general was needed. Hoche had already excluded himelf by his political clumsiness, so the only other available general of comparable prestige was Bonaparte. The latter dispatched General Augereau with a division, who eliminated the "black collars" in the coup d'etat of 18 Fructidor (4 September 1797). The party favoring further territorial expansion now had the upper hand in Paris and Bonaparte had no further fear of being disavowed for his conquests.

The so-called treaty of Campo Formio (18 October 1797) was in fact signed at Passariano, where Bonaparte and Josephine were holding court. The Directory was quite satisfied, for Austria not only abandoned Belgium to France but, in secret articles, recognized the French claim to the entire left bank of the Rhine. Bonaparte, on the other hand, viewing the treaty from the Italian perspective, was not displeased, for Austria ceded Lombardy to France, and Venice lost its territories (except for the Ionian islands).

French opinion largely approved, as did the partisans of the principles of 1789 who lived in occupied and conquered territories or in neighboring Germany, particularly the Rhenish states. Bonaparte was certainly saluted as a victorious soldier, but even more as the man who brought peace to a continent where war had raged for more than five years. This was proof, if proof were needed, that people everywhere wanted peace.

Bonaparte had certainly appreciated the strength of the peace-loving sentiment that he had encountered throughout this period. However, as neither he nor his government could conceive of any other peace than that imposed by a victorious France (the continental powers and England naturally had a different conception) the result for Europe could mean only another eighteen years of almost uninterrupted war. For the moment, though, Bonaparte, and not the Directory, got the credit for the peace.

The Italian war was decisive in the formation and evolution of Bonaparte. For the first time, he held in his own hands military, political, diplomatic, and even financial power. Therefore he became not only a figure of crucial importance in domestic French politics, but also a changed man.

Bonaparte wished to give to both the republics that he founded in Italy a constitution modeled on that of the Year III, but seeing that the Fructidor coup had demonstrated that this system was not working brilliantly in France, Napoleon recognized that it would be hard to fob off on the Cisalpine Republic. He expressed his views on this in a letter to Talleyrand, minister of foreign affairs in Paris. It was important in both countries, he wrote, not to permit the legislative branch to encroach on the authority of the executive, thus requiring the intervention of bayonets to save the day, as at Fructidor. Until the right constitution could be put in place, he had tried, he told Talleyrand, to create institutions in Italy where the public offices were filled directly by him, not by election. The appointees were by and large moderates, either aristocrats or bourgeois, and not left-wing "anarchists" or clerical "ultras," dominated by priests. He was surprised by the degree of anti-French reaction that he encountered, as much among educated people sincerely attached to the principles of the Revolution as among the lower classes aroused by "their monks." Bonaparte in truth did not understand that what he was confronting were the first manifestations of an Italian patriotism hostile to foreigners. He did not see that an Italian could be sincerely Jacobin and yet also opposed to the excesses of the French occupation. In short, he committed the same error he would repeat later in Spain, Germany, and Russia: he underestimated the importance of national sentiment among defeated peoples.

Bonaparte had enjoyed a leisurely initiation into the art of diplomacy and had displayed real talent for it at Tolentino and Campo Formio. The Directory had desired Belgium and the Rhine. He took the first, had every expectation of obtaining the second, and seized northern Italy. He had not, therefore (as some later reproached him for) sacrificed the Rhine to Italy, for the former eventually became French, and the French had Bonaparte to thank. Yet the adulation afforded the peacemaker of Europe sometimes made people forget the grave danger of impending war.

First, France's principal adversary, England, had not the slightest intention of recognizing the annexation of Belgium. This attitude only encouraged the Austrians to take up arms again at the first opportunity to attempt retake Milan. Austria, not wishing to implicate the Holy Roman Empire in the Treaty of Campo Formio, decided to open a congress at Rastadt, where the princes of the empire would decide how to divide war indemnities and compensate their Rhenish colleagues dispossessed by the French annexations. These highly delicate negotiations could easily create further continental complications. Finally, by installing France in Italy through the creation of vassal states, Bonaparte had completely exceeded the so-called doctrine of France's "natural frontiers," thereby engaging his adopted country in an Italian—even a Mediterranean, and indeed even a Near Eastern—policy that could not but put peace at serious risk.

Bonaparte had by now become an indispensable element in French internal politics. His pillaging in Italy had permitted the regime to surmount the financial crisis, while during Fructidor he had assured its political survival. If, at the time of Vendemiaire, he had become the executor of the wills of the Thermidorians, henceforth he treated with them as an equal, securely tied to the regime by the same community of interests.

In fact, since Lodi his gaze was turned steadfastly on Paris. Well he knew how unpopular the Directory had become, and well he sensed that power lay there for the taking, provided only that one could reassure the beneficiaries of the Revolution that they would not lose what they had gained. With rare mastery he now moved to win the favor of his army and his country. He sought to convince the public, not merely the few hundred thousand eligible voters, of the magnitude of his victories and the universality of his genius. With money extracted from the Italians, he published newspapers of various political shades—*Le Courrier de l'Armée d'Italie, Le Patriote Français à Milan* (somewhat Jacobin), and *La France Vue de l'Armée d'Italie* (rather moderate)—that were distributed freely to the army and even widely read in France. These papers adroitly played on the themes of the young general's simplicity, of his aversion to dictatorship, his dislike of luxury, the plainness of his manners—all contracting sharply with the spectacle offered by the Directorial regime. Propaganda of word was matched by propaganda of image as, after 1796, the great painter Gros made Bonaparte famous with his portrait of the victor of Arcola.

Was the real man much like the image he purveyed? The poor officer of the spartan lifestyle had, on the contrary, amassed a spectacular fortune of dubious origins. The confiscation of the mines of Idria, alone, had brought him a million francs [5 million dollars in today's currency]. He had developed a taste for luxury and conspicuous consumption, and maintained a brilliant court at Montebello. It was indeed difficult to imagine that he would ever agree to return to being just a general. "I no longer know how to obey," he admitted on returning to Paris.

3. The Egyptian Campaign
(1798–1799)

On 26 and 27 October 1797, the Directory commissioned Bonaparte to resolve the two great remaining problems of French foreign policy: the question of war, on which turned his nomination as commander in chief of the Army of England, and the final disposition of the Rhenish territory, on which hung Bonaparte's designation as plenipoteniary at Rastadt. He arrived at Rastadt on 26 November and on 1 December signed a secret convention with the Austrian delegates that provided that imperial (German) troops would evacuate Mainz and the French would withdraw from the Venetian territories. On the 5th of the month Bonaparte was back in Paris preparing for war against England.

The challenge lay in massing French naval forces in the English Channel long enough to safely transport an invading army to England. But an inspection of the French fleet (8 to 20 February) convinced Bonaparte of the pitiful condition of the navy. Because he was not the sort of general who would risk his reputation on a campaign of dubious promise, he presented the Directory with a report advising against a direct invasion of England, and suggesting instead an attack in Hanover or in Egypt. On the other hand, there was little chance of attacking Hanover without risking a war with all the imperial states—at the very time when peace negotiations at Rastadt were attempting to settle relations between France and the empire. And as for Egypt, it was officially a colony of the Ottoman Turks, who were neither an ally of the British nor an enemy of the French.

Still, the idea of an Egyptian expedition hung in the air. As early as 1796, the French consul in Cairo had pressed for an occupation of the country. On 3 July 1797, Talleyrand read a memorandum to the French Institute in which he advocated that the French acquire Egypt as compensation for losing the Antilles. In sum, little by little the idea gained ground in official French circles to seize Egypt as a means of menacing Britain directly, by aiding Tippo-Sahib in his revolt against English forces in the East Indies, and indirectly, as a generalized threat to India. These were ideas which Bonaparte made his own.

Thus, on 5 March 1798, the Directory formally ordered Bonaparte to undertake the conquest of Egypt. Did the government secretly wish, as Napoleon would later claim, to "exile" an overly ambitious general? This is rather unlikely; what government would risk 40,000 men and its last fleet merely to get rid of a worrisome general? In truth, all sides in Paris political circles could agree on one thing: to bring England to her knees. Thus did the Egyptian expeditionary force become known unofficially as the "left flank of the Army of England."

A fleet of 65 men-of-war and 280 troop transports was assembled at Toulon, Civita-Vecchia, Genoa, and in Corsica. It carried 38,000 men, 1,200 horses, and 171 cannon, including a scientific mission of some 200 savants and artists. For the first time Bonaparte would display a fault in his military genius: his neglect of climate. In mid-July, his men disembarked for a campaign in Egypt rigged out in gear intended for winter warfare in Europe.

After reprovisioning itself on 19 May, the expedition surrounded Malta, conquered it, and occupied it on 6 June. By the first of the next month, the French were at Alexandria. Without a declaration of war, they attacked and trounced the Turkish garrison, replacing it with 3,000

French soldiers under the command of General Kléber. With the rest of the army, Bonaparte marched on Cairo, while the fleet entered the Nile. Turkish Mameluke cavalry attacked the army on 21 July, but their charges were repulsed and broken by French infantry squares massed by Bonaparte at the foot of the Pyramids. For lack of cavalry, the French could not pursue and destroy the entire Mameluke force; nevertheless, on the 23rd the Army of Egypt entered Cairo. Little more than a week later, Lord Nelson utterly destroyed the French fleet of Admiral Brueys, anchored in Alexandria harbor.

The Directory next ordered Bonaparte to send 15,000 troops from the port of Suez to support the revolt of Tippo-Sahib in the East Indies. Before doing this, however, he had to ensure his own dominance in Egypt, which consumed six more months. Arriving in Suez in December 1798, Bonaparte did not find enough vessels to transport the men, and in any case the issue was academic, for Tippo-Sahib had been defeated and killed.

In strictly military terms, the expedition to Egypt was a total defeat: the French army was blockaded in its conquered territory, and England remained mistress of the Mediterranean, its hold on the Indies reinforced. But the expedition also had unfortunate consequences in Europe. In September 1798, Turkey had declared war on France, and, soon after, had taken the unusual step of authorizing the Russian tsar, Paul I, to send his fleet through the Dardanelles into the Mediterranean. In December England, Naples, and Russia concluded an alliance to make an armed intervention in Italy. Austria, though formally neutral, authorized the passage of Russian troops through its territories, so the Directory declared war on her as well (12 March 1799).

As he had in Italy, so now in Egypt, Bonaparte sought to win over at least the holders of local power to his cause, and on their behalf he busied himself with organization, administration, and legislation. But because he refused to renounce exploiting the country, he failed to win any hearts and minds.

On 2 July, he presented himself to the Egyptian population as its liberator, while affirming his intention to respect the Koran, for he dearly wished to avoid religious difficulties. Three days later he launched a veritable mass appeal for revolt against the Mameluke governors, but to his great surprise the country did not budge. Almost on the next day he fell back on the familiar policy of imposing heavy gold and silver tributes on the Alexandrian merchants. Realizing the impossibility of direct French governancy of so large a country, he set up in each city a "divan" of notables, whom he charged with overseeing administration, provisioning, and policing, under the general control of French commissioners. But kept in place the local system of justice and taxation.

To promote the research of the savants and scientists who had accompanied him, Bonaparte decided on 22 August to found a sort of branch office of the Paris-based French Institute. This was the Egyptian Institute, to which he assigned no less a mission than "the progress and propagation of the [mainly French] philosophers [*Lumières*] in Egypt," and studies of the natural resources and history of the country. If the first part of the assignment was a failure, we owe to the second most of the documentation that undergirds the modern discipline of Egyptology. In accordance with the views of the Directory, Bonaparte ordered a study of ways to improve navigation in the Nile, more particularly to restore the ancient connection between the river and the Red Sea. He also ordered studies of ways to purify the water of the Nile and improve local sanitation. Although his goal was to protect his soldiers from epidemics, these measures improved health conditions for the Egyptians. This policy had no major immediate effect, but it made a key contribution to the economic growth of the country.

The many oppressions of occupation were nonetheless insupportable to the indigenous peoples, and as conditions worsened, the sultan declared a holy war against the French. Beginning in September 1798, uprisings broke out, followed by bloody reprisals.

Because England planned to attack Egypt with two Turkish armies, one disembarking to the west of the Nile delta, the other marching from Syria, Bonaparte took his men northeast. The Syrian expedition quit Cairo in February 1799. Desert and disease decimated an already inadequate force of 15,000 men that lacked siege artillery. The French nevertheless took El Arish (21 February), while Gaza gave up without a fight. Jaffa, energetically defended by the mamelukes, fell on 7 March; 2,000 Turkish soldiers and numerous civilians were massacred. But Bonaparte could not take Saint Jean d'Acre, stubbornly defended by the emigre French commander, Phélippeaux, a classmate from Brienne. He fell back on Egypt, returning in time to throw into the sea a Turkish army disembarked at Aboukir (25 July). This success enabled him to sail victoriously for France even though the army remained blockaded in Egypt.

On 22 August, Bonaparte turned over command to Kléber, and had read to the army an order of the day that announced that the former general in chief was leaving for France, but for only a short absence. Can one fairly charge him with abandonment of post in time of war? No, if it is recalled that on 26 May, the Directory had ordered the expedition to return. Yes, if it is kept in mind that Bonaparte left before receiving this word and indeed without even knowing it was coming.

CHAPTER 2

From General to Emperor

1. Brumaire: A Civilian Coup d'Etat Staged by a Soldier

*T*he coup d'etat that permitted Bonaparte to accede to power was not only an act perpetrated by a popular general for his own profit, it was also well prepared by an aspiring bourgeoisie heartily tired of having the advantages it had won from the Revolution jeopardized again and again by the inability of a weak regime to wield power and guarantee stability. It was also prepared by certain men, among them some of the most important in the Directory, who dreamed, not of gaining power, but of continuing to hold it. For the coup was accomplished with the crucial participation of two of the five Directors and with the complicity of the Council of Elders, all of whom wished to avoid violence and bloodshed. For these people, Bonaparte was merely the executor of their designs.

In fact, a coup was decided upon because it was impossible to revise the Constitution of the Year III by legal means before 1805. The principal fault of the constitution was that it did not ensure the equilibrium of powers, but separated too absolutely the legislative from the executive without providing for resolving conflicts between them. Every year, moreover, one director and a third of the members of the two houses were elected—a provision that kept the country in a state of continuous agitation. From the outset the Directory had been a target for the former members of the Mountain (the radical, anti-monarchist party of the Convention, 1791–1794), as well as for the royalists who reappeared after the Terror. To remain in power, the Thermidorians, who were mostly regicides, had used small coups d'etat: against the royalists on 18 Fructidor, and against the Jacobins on 22 Floreal. On each occasion the executive was trying to purge a legitimately elected majority from the legislature. But on 30 Prairial VII, an alliance between the left and the right oppositions gave the legislature its revenge: three directors were forced to resign.

By now the entire directorial regime was in disrepute because of this ongoing political anarchy, not to mention the government's inability to relieve France's economic and financial difficulties. French armies were poorly equipped, roads were poorly maintained, brigandage was rife in the countryside, and the nation was outraged by rampant corruption and immorality in high state positions, a corruption that stood in sharp contrast with the misery of the population.

Meanwhile the campaigns of the second coalition had begun disastrously. In the spring of 1799, Italy was lost to Suvorov's offensive, and Switzerland and Holland were invaded (the latter by an Anglo-Russian force). French frontiers were threatened from upper Alsace to the Alps.

Even so, the Directory attempted to redress the situation, politically as well as militarily. A reform project was implemented, beginning with the fiscal reform (whose fruits the Consulate would reap) that established a corps of specialized state functionaries and envisioned four forms of direct taxation (land, head and movables, excise, and a "doors and windows" tax). Public assistance to the poor was instituted, as well as a plan to improve roads and the navigability of rivers. Measures were also taken to promote commerce and industry. On the military front, the victories of Brune at Bergen (19 September 1799) and Masséna at Zurich (25 to 27 September) saved France from invasion. The coalition fell apart when the tsar withdrew his armies. Nevertheless public opinion gave the regime no credit for these achievements; on the contrary, the revival of Jacobinism and royalism spread anxiety among moderate republicans.

After the parliamentary victory of Prairial, measures were taken that seemed to the new holders of property to be an echo of the Terror: forced loans were imposed on the wealthy, a new law on hostages was aimed at Catholic priests and the relatives of emigres (the former nobility and their families). The Jourdan Law of 1797, which set up military conscription, was immediately followed by a draft of five classes of conscripts, allowing for no exceptions or replacements, a measure the bourgeoisie found odious. On 14 July, Jourdan went so far as to propose a toast to "the revival of the pikes," a reference to the weapons carried by the sans-culottes at the height of the Revolution (1792–1794). Nor was the royalist menace any less real. A right-wing insurrection erupted on 5 August in Haute-Garonne, and, though quickly repressed, spread to the Gers and the Ariège. Then, in mid-October, the west broke into revolt again.

Thus did the conservative bourgeoisie long for an authoritative regime that would reinforce executive power and bring a definite finish to the Revolution, as well as consolidate the Revolution's material gains (nationalized church land, called *biens nationaux*), and political reforms (national sovereignty) at the expense of the royalists and Jacobins. The bourgeoisie's revisionist aspirations, increasingly shared by public opinion, now became focused on a small group of ambitious intriguers who, for two years, had been scheming to bring about a coup. This group inhabited the salons, notably that of Madame de Staël. It included men such as Benjamin Constant, Barras, Lucien Bonaparte (who was president of the Council of Five Hundred), and Siéyès. Their (often contradictory) plans and ideas began to attract capitalists hostile to the forced loans, Ideologues of the Institute, and sundry generals increasingly caught up in politics. At the center of this intrigue stood Siéyès, now a Director, who sought to blend national sovereignty with a strong, stable executive. He envisioned substituting executive co-optation for popular election. This would institutionalize the politics of decree and purge that the Directory had been carrying out since Fructidor.

A coup d'etat was the only means of realizing Siéyès's plan. He convinced two other Directors, Barras and Roger-Ducos, that the army would force the project through the legislature, as had happened in Fructidor. The army was keenly feeling the effects of the duration and the bloodiness of the war. Soldiers and officers alike despised the politicians who could not pay, feed, or equip them properly. Generals now talked openly of freeing themselves from civil authority, and indeed did so as they conducted military operations, made diplomatic negotiations, and administered conquered territory. They became more and more intrigued by the political game in Paris. In the Year VII alone, fourteen of them proposed themselves for the post of Director.

For Siéyès, the choice of which "sword" to rely on was not easy. He needed a general who could order a republican army to act against a no less republican legislature (both houses were purged of royalists in Fructidor) and yet not wish to take a major political role for himself afterwards. His first choice was Joubert, a moderate and a staunch adversary of the Jacobins. But because he was a soldier with a less illustrious military reputation than other generals, Joubert was instead given command of the Army of Italy in the hope that he would garner additional glory. As it happened, he was killed at Novi on 15 August 1799. Siéyès was considering Moreau when Bonaparte landed at Fréjus from Egypt (9 October).

It first seemed that the Corsican had left Egypt in the hope of reconquering Italy. Public opinion welcomed him, saw him as the man who would win further victories and restore peace in Europe. All the way from Fréjus to Paris (where he arrived on 16 October), the warmth of the popular greeting given Bonaparte impressed him deeply with his own standing in the nation's eyes. Convinced that Jacobinism had no future, and instinctively hostile to royalism, he used the contacts of his brothers Joseph and Lucien to draw closer to the revisionist camp of moderates. He did not intend that any future government would reap the prestige of re-establishing peace without his participation.

A meeting between Siéyès and Bonaparte, with Talleyrand acting as mediator, brought the situation to a climax. An agreement between them was not easily arrived at, but

Siéyès knew he needed a general with a left-wing reputation whom the army would unhesitatingly follow.

A shrewd campaign was launched in the newspapers linking peace with a change of constitution. To render the latter indispensable, the threat of a royalist restoration was brandished against liberty, and that of a social revolution, against property. Money was needed to enflame the zeal of generals and soldiers. As bankers were proving hesitant to support the plotters, funds were raised from suppliers of arms and materiel to the army, who were annoyed at a recent law abolishing the privileged status of their invoices with the state treasury. Three Directors could be counted on: Siéyès, of course; Barras, now neutralized; and Roger-Ducos, who did not especially care about the outcome. Most of the Elders were won over to the coup, while the Five Hundred were presided over by Lucien Bonaparte. According to Siéyès's plan, the appearance of legality would be maintained because both houses would formally approve the revision. Bonaparte was to play only a secondary part, that of defender of republican institutions threatened by Jacobin conspiracy.

On 18 Brumaire in the Year VIII (9 November 1799), the Elders, excluding the known opponents of Siéyès's scheme, who were "overlooked", were convoked for 7:00 A.M. at the Tuileries. The deputy Cornet read a report denouncing the Jacobin plot. The Elders then voted for the transfer of both houses to Saint-Cloud, which the constitution permitted. They charged Bonaparte with the execution of this decree. To do this, he was given command of the garrison of Paris, a perfectly legal measure, within the Directory's competence. It now remained only to obtain the Directors' resignations. Siéyès and Roger-Ducos offered theirs forthwith, Barras let himself be convinced with the offer of a comfortable "indemnity," and Gohier and Moulin (held under house arrest at the Luxembourg Palace by Moreau) finally conceded defeat. Posters were displayed all over Paris. Some attacked the Directors personally: "Their actions have effectively destroyed the constitution!" Others said simply, "Citizens, Bonaparte must be in Paris if we are to have peace."

All was calm in the capital, where the stock exchange began to climb out of a low. However, the night of the 18th gave the Jacobins a chance to rally, so that one of Bonaparte's agents, Cambacérès, fearing a failure, began to plan a further coup. Indeed, the conspirators still faced the most difficult part of their task: imposing constitutional revision on the legislature. As late as 19 Brumaire a commission to consider revision had still not been named. In the end, the plan would fail because of Bonaparte.

On the 19th, he arrived unexpectedly at Saint-Cloud with 5,000 soldiers. Alarmed at the presence of so many troops, some of the deputies wavered. In the Elders' meeting hall, the "overlooked" of the day before were now on hand, fervently trying to convince their compatriots of the dubious reality of any Jacobin plot. Under the circumstances, the majority now hesitated to constitute a new executive to place the resigned Directory. Meanwhile, in the Council of Five Hundred, the left had used a roll-call vote to force all the deputies to renew their oath of loyalty to the constitution. Things seemed to be dragging, so Bonaparte decided to help them along.

He entered the meeting hall of the Elders in the midst of their discussion of the proposal to name a provisional government. There he launched himself on a tangled and incoherent discourse that won him nothing and left his partisans weakened. Next, with several other generals and a grenadier escort, he went to the Council of Five Hundred, where he was welcomed with cries of "Outlaw!" and "Down with the tyrant!" Half-fainting, jostled by a few incensed deputies, Bonaparte was extracted from the melee with difficulty by his soldiers. All seemed lost.

The Five Hundred, however, by threatening to proscribe the plotters, succeeded only in driving them from their ostensibly legal stance to violence. It was Lucien who turned the situation around. By adjourning the Council, he prevented them from declaring his brother an outlaw. Meanwhile, Napoleon was having very little success convincing his troops that the deputies wished to kill their commander. Lucien, on horseback, now joined him in the courtyard and harangued the grenadiers charged with guarding the Council. As president of the Five Hundred, he embodied the law in their eyes. He denounced the minority of "representatives of the dagger . . . undoubtedly in the pay of England" who wished to kill Napoleon and he dramatically proclaimed his passion for liberty, even if it should lead him to act against his own brother. Finally the grenadiers of Murat and Leclerc acted: they entered the Orangerie and expelled deputies and spectators alike.

Immediately afterward, the conspirators returned to formally adhering to the niceties of legal appearances. Deputies from the Elders and the Five Hundred were now enticed out of hiding in the woods around Saint-Cloud and put to deliberating by the light of candles. Finally, about 2:00 A.M., the Elders created a provisional executive consular commission, comprising Bonaparte, Siéyès, Roger-Ducos— to be known as Consuls of the French Republic—and charged them with the plenitude of power formerly held by the Directory. At the same time the two houses purged themselves by eliminating sixty-two deputies judged guilty of "excesses and attempted crimes," and then adjourned *sine die*, naming in their place two commissions of their own members charged with preparing a new constitution. The new regime, however, must "hold inviolable the sovereignty of the people, the one and indivisible Republic, the representative system, the division of powers, and liberty, equality, security, and property."

In Paris the crowd, believing the war would soon end, was shouting "Long live peace!", while the soldiers, certain that their actions had saved it, were shouting "Long live the Republic!" In short, the coup was accomplished with considerable equivocation.

Intended as parliamentary, the coup now became military because of the blundering of Bonaparte, whose hesitation before the Five Hundred made the army's intervention necessary and decisive. Siéyès was thus momentarily supplanted by Bonaparte as chief protagonist, but as Bonaparte could not really play the role effectively, the initiative soon returned to Siéyès, as well as to Lucien Bonaparte and Murat, who were responsible for the actual execution. For the politicians who prepared the coup, 18 and 19 Brumaire would each come to be called a "Day of the Duped," as the real beneficiary presently emerged.

2. The Legacy: Disorder, Revolution, War

The purpose of the Brumaire coup was clear: putting an end to a regime that was undoubtedly excessively derided but that had nevertheless brought the country to the brink of anarchy, bankruptcy, and the corruption of public morality. On 20 November 1799, the state coffers held not more than 167,000 francs in hard currency, but leading Paris bankers now agreed to a loan of 12 million francs, thus associating high finance with the new regime.

In many regions of France all authority had disappeared. In the west, 40,000 Chouans held the countryside, blocking passage and communication between the capital and the western seaboard. Roving bands extorted money from frightened citizens throughout the valley of the Rhone, Provence, Languedoc, and the right bank of the Garonne. Travelers were attacked and robbed. The homes of rich "patriots" were pillaged. Belgium, recently annexed, broke out in open insurrection, thus stopping trade and communication with Holland. All this, as well as heavy taxation, the "indelicacies" of the soldiery, and the anti-Catholic laws provoked strong discontent. When conscription was enforced, the peasants, supported by their clergy, revolted.

Throughout the Republic, the economy was badly depressed. In Lyon, for example, silk weavers now numbered 1,500 instead of 8,000, as in 1789. In Paris, workshops could employ only one worker of every eight. Roads were impassable; bridges, out. Bonaparte well understood that the country wanted above all a government capable of restoring prosperity and assuring public order.

The provisional consuls took it as a sacred charge to guarantee the political conquests of the Revolution. As long as this was assured, public opinion was relatively indifferent to the form of the future government. Republican zeal had cooled, and it was with much difficulty that republican candidates were found to fill public offices. But his surface indifference covered the visceral attachment of most Frenchmen to the civil conquests of the Revolution, and most especially to the idea of social equality. All the beneficiaries of the Revolution—peasant and bourgeois owners of church lands, public functionaries, and of course the men who had voted the death of the late king—lived in great fear of any restoration of the Old Regime. And the spectre of a Jacobin republic haunted the dreams of all property holders.

Thus, Bonaparte's ambition was served by the anxiety of his countrymen, eager to enjoy their recently acquired advantages. He understood that the French people would allow a certain amount of cheating on principles as long as their interests were protected. He also grasped that this required him not to identify himself with any political party.

Paradoxically, Bonaparte understood that the popular hopes that carried him to power wished him to conclude peace, but a peace that conserved for France its Belgian, Rhenish, and Italian acquisitions. However, he did not have the power to decide these matters on his own. On the very day that he was installed as one of three consuls, he sent messages to the English king and German emperor inviting them to work with him for the restoration of peace. But they did not reply, thus proving that the European monarchies were still not disposed to accept a France headed by a son of the Revolution. The war was economic as well as military, and the Directory, under the cover of the conflict with England, had inaugurated a policy aimed at establishing French economic hegemony throughout Europe. Was it now possible to go backwards without angering the French manufacturing bourgeoisie? Though chief of state, Bonaparte would spend more time in the company of his armies than in the palaces of government.

The new consul was all the more condemned to succeed because he was burdened by difficulties about the way
in which he had risen to power, difficulties that would dog
him to 1815. He was, first, the object of the jealousy of all
the other generals—Moreau, Bernadotte, Augereau, etc.—
who each believed that he could have brought off the coup
d'etat at least as well as Bonaparte. Then he had to deal
with the Jacobins, who accused him of violating national
sovereignty to make himself a tyrant. Next came the royalists who, the moment they recognized that a monarchical
restoration was not in the offing, attacked Bonaparte as a
usurper. Finally, he had to cope with the hostility of the
very men of Brumaire who had called on him to help execute the coup but who had not intended that this general
be its principal beneficiary and despot of France. In sum,
intrigues, plots, and attempted assassinations would accom-
pany Bonaparte throughout the years of power. Rarely has
a chief of state exercised his functions in such dangerous
conditions.

3. The Installation of the New Regime

The men of Brumaire took power in order to give France a
new constitution. After the coup (9 to 10 November) and
before the document was completed (25 December 1799),
Bonaparte succeeded in overcoming them. By good fortune,
it was decided that each provisional consul would preside,
seriatim, over the government, and that they would serve
in alphabetical order. Bonaparte thus held preeminence at
the outset. The consuls chose the ministers. The holdovers
from the previous regime included Cambacérès at Justice

and Fouché at Police; the new men called to office included Berthier at War and Gaudin (a remarkable technician) at Finance. Bonaparte understood that his popularity could not be maintained unless the government restored public confidence.

He took great pains to disassociate himself from the extremes: "neither red bonnets nor red slippers!" He reassured the large financial interests because the state had need of their means. The forced loans were replaced by a 25 percent increase in the three main sources of taxation. He solemnly promised "a government of social defense that would be a friend of order, respectful of property in all its forms, and peaceful in its foreign policy."

Bonaparte also assured himself of the cooperation of two recently victorious generals, Masséna and Brune. His government hit at the left and at the right. A certain number of Jacobins were proscribed, but Bonaparte cleverly let Fouché take the responsibility for this, while taking credit himself for rallying some well-known republicans, such as General Jourdan. The law forbidding emigres to return was retained.

In a time of great expectations, Bonaparte thus pushed himself forward in the public eye at the expense of the other plotters of Brumaire. Yet he needed to transform this moral ascendance into a legally defined political preeminence. This he would accomplish with the Constitution of the Year VIII.

Siéyès and the Ideologues were sufficiently powerful in the two legislative commissions that no move to establish a despotism could come from this direction. They wished, rather, to consolidate the preeminence of the bourgeoisie of speculators in nationalized lands and of war profiteers, the men who had held power since 1795. They desired a continuation of a representative regime, but one that would not fall into the excesses of parliamentarism or popular sovereignty. They wished to get rid of their more embarrassing colleagues from the Directory without instituting dictatorship. To accomplish this, they favored a collegial executive. At the head of state would be a grand elector, appointed for life but with a purely representative function. He, in turn, would designate two consuls, one for internal affairs, the other for foreign policy. Real power would reside in a College of Conservatives (College des Conservateurs), or Senate, recruited by co-optation, which would choose from among the notables the members of the legislative houses as well as name the grand elector. The latter, though appointed for life, could be removed by the College (Senate). In short, this created an oligarchy of the notables.

Such a plan hardly conformed to the aspirations of Bonaparte, who made it known that he, for one, had no desire to be "a fattening pig" at the public trough. He sensed that the real power would reside more convincingly in a man who drew his support from popular consent expressed directly in a plebiscite. Siéyès was forced to agree to this reinforcement of executive power and its concentration in Bonaparte's hands. The new constitution placed at the head of state three consuls, named by the Senate to ten-year terms that were indefinitely renewable. The First Consul, who was not responsible to the legislature, alone held the law-making and law-enforcing initiative. Because he also named the ministers and nearly all state functionaries, he was all-powerful at the local level as well. The only powers denied him were the right to declare war and the right to make peace. The other two consuls had merely consultative roles. The constitution further granted the First Consul a collegial supporting body called the Conseil d'Etat (Council of State), whose function was to draft legislation and regulations, and to hand down rulings in administrative conflicts. The regulatory and administrative power held by this council would prevail over legislative power and render it illusory. It was the vital mainspring of the new executive and was beyond all legislative control.

It was stipulated that the names of the first group of three consuls would actually appear in the text of the constitution and that they would be chosen by the commissions set up following the dissolution of the legislature after the coup d'etat. After the vote was taken, but before it could be counted, Bonaparte flung the ballots into the fire and invited Siéyès to choose the First Consul. This was of course merely a show, for it had already been agreed that he would select Bonaparte, with Cambacérès and Lebrun (Bonaparte's men) as Second and Third Consuls. Cambacérès would occupy himself with judicial matters; Lebrun, with finances. It was another instance of Bonaparte protecting himself on both the right and the left, for Cambacérès was a regicide, whereas Lebrun had been a close collaborator of Maupeou (a leading minister of Louis XV).

Because Bonaparte wished to anchor his authority in popular consent, the constitution was submitted to a plebiscite, the only sign that universal suffrage was not a complete illusion under the new regime. This procedure would be used again in 1802, 1804, and 1815, for in reality Bonaparte's system was nothing but an autocracy with a plebiscitary base. To Napoleon, inviting the people to pronounce on the question of the new constitution was to place himself squarely in the revolutionary tradition of the convention. It also meant avoiding, by passing over the heads of, the two intermediary commissions, which could thus no longer exercise their function of "preventing authority from becoming despotism." To hold power from the people, at least in appearance, was for Napoleon a way of by-passing the tutelage of the men of Brumaire, but this did not mean that he actually intended to govern with the popular classes, whom he mistrusted, though he instinctively understood their aspirations. Hence his recourse to the plebiscite. He knew, too, from the police that the cheers with which he had been greeted on his return from Egypt had already begun to die down; thus he took certain precautions to win a favorable result in the plebiscite.

Citizens were invited to inscribe a yes or a no in the voting registers available in their town halls or other local meeting places. Arbitrarily, the consuls decided that a majority yes vote in Paris would suffice to put the constitution into effect. This was achieved on 24 December 1799, when the capital's response was known 32,440 in favor, 14 opposed). Six more weeks passed before the result was published nationally. In all, out of approximately 5 million eligible voters, it was reported that 3,011,117 voted yes and 1,562 voted no. Thanks to the work of Charles Langlois, we now know, however, that Lucien Bonaparte, serving as Minister of the Interior, arbitrarily raised the reported number of votes by 900,000 all of which of course were counted as yesses. In reality, therefore, the constitution was approved by only a minority of eligible French voters, hardly the enthusiastic popular approbation that Bonaparte had sought. By cheating on the election, Lucien once again saved his brother. The majority of Frenchmen remained hesitant; the new regime enjoyed the favor of only the minority who had voted. In escaping from the despotism of the parliamentary Directory, the nation thus rested its fate in the hands of a man who claimed to embody both the national will and the authority of the state. The nation consented to Bonapartism, but it did not adhere to it enthusiastically.

4. Citizen Bonaparte, First Consul

It is nonetheless true that the thirty-year-old man whom the painter David sketched for posterity, portraying him as slender, plainly coiffed, and rather unkempt, possessed the qualities needed to fulfill the nation's deepest aspirations. He had already shown his value on the battlefield, demonstrated in Italy and Egypt exceptional qualities as an administrator and statesman, and acquired valuable experience in public affairs. For all that, he was not omniscient. For example, he had no profound grasp of financial and economic issues. But at least he was aware of what he did not know, and he did not fail to ask for advice from those who would know. He even listened to what they had to say, at least in the beginning. He mistrusted theory, going straight to the practical side of problems. "My policy," he would say, "is to govern men as the majority of them wish to be governed." A man of action, not of doctrine, he knew how to adapt his solutions to changing political, economic, and social conditions, though the adaptations that seemed wise to him were not always the best solutions.

His correspondence reveals that few things escaped his attention. Taking as much interest in verifying the effectiveness of a regiment as in knowing what was in the state treasury, Bonaparte, possessed of exceptional physical energy, would exhaust his assistants and entourage, going from one thorny problem to the next with a facility that impressed experts with his quick insight. Was it a good thing that the chief of state had his nose in every detail? Perhaps, for if intelligent associates were not lacking to Bonaparte, rare indeed were those in whom he could blindly trust, and therefore he was partly justified in giving his subordinates little initiative.

Except on the field of battle, where Napoleon sometimes met the unexpected with strokes of pure genius, he tended to give each problem that arose the exact measure of consideration that its importance deserved, no more, no less. For a long time, his greatest strength lay in intuiting what was possible and not possible, in finding the most audacious combinations in only those enterprises that had the best chances of success. As the years went by, he would change, of course, but this faculty of adaptation to circumstances, of improvising in changing situations, of finding multiple paths around every obstacle, and (not least) his taste for action and for wielding authority would make of him a man with no common measure in the world or ordinary men. Whence his strength, and his weakness.

5. Stabilizing the Revolution in France

When they took up their duties, the three consuls announced, "Citizens, the Revolution, anchored in those principles with which she began, is now finished!" This meant a return to 1791, the period that saw the dismantling of absolutism and of the society of the ancien regime, but not to the radical phase that followed (1792–1794). In the France of 1799, such a decision required new institutions.

The Reorganization of Institutions

The Napoleonic regime always remained true to the principle of national sovereignty. Popular consent was the foundation of its legitimacy. Once the Constitution of the Year VIII re-established universal (male) suffrage, no further Napoleonic constitution would deprive the citizen of that right, though the right to vote should not be confused with the right to elect. It was rather the right to draw up lists of the eligible—men legally empowered to exercise representative and administrative functions.

The representative system was conserved, but at the cost of considerably weakening the legislative power. The two assemblies, the Tribunate and the Legislative Body, competed in the drafting of law, but, because their members were not directly elected, they had no anchor in national sovereignty, hence no recourse against the First Consul, who brought them increasingly under his subjection with constitutional modifications. In short, the legislative power had no control over the executive. Deprived of initiative, the assemblies could not even amend government bills drawn up by the Council of State. Furthermore, those representatives in the Tribunate who debated bills were not the same as those in the Legislative Body who voted on them. All control over political life had been stripped from these bodies.

But a new power did make its appearance, the Senate, stronghold of the men of Brumaire and of the regime. It named the members of the two assemblies and it named the three consuls, whose acts it could quash as unconstitutional. Being itself neither elected nor even designated by an outside body (it recruited new members by co-optation) the Senate depended on no one but controlled everything.

This was a completely new institution whose members, once in place, could not be removed and enjoyed high salaries (over $100,000 in modern currency). They might have opposed the power of the executive if they had not let themselves become domesticated by Bonaparte.

The First Consul named the ministers. Two of them (Lucien Bonaparte at Interior and Talleyrand at Foreign Affairs) were original men of Brumaire, one (Fouché, at Police) had rallied to Brumaire, one (Berthier, at War) was a revolutionary general, and one (Gaudin, at Finance) had served the Old Regime, though he had also served in the treasury under the Legislative Assembly and the convention. Bonaparte also named the twenty-nine members of the Council of State, of whom twenty had been elected to one or another of the revolutionary assemblies. In conformity with the constitution, Siéyès presided over the choice of the first group of twenty-nine senators who, with Siéyès himself and Roger-Ducos, constituted a majority of thirty-one that then co-opted the other twenty-nine members. The sixty senators, in their turn, designated the 100 members of the Tribunate and the 300 members of the Legislative Body. Despite the presence of a few outsiders of particular merit or distinction—such scientists as Berthollet, Monge, Leplace, and Volney, a revolutionary general such as Kellermann, or a few camouflaged royalists—the preponderance of these appointments went to men who had served in the various revolutionary assemblies, mostly from the old "plain" of the convention—regicides of Thermidor, repentant men of the Terror.

The constitution fulfilled the wishes both of Bonaparte and the men of Brumaire, and the later constitutional evolution of the regime would reflect the rapport between

them. As the First Consul insisted on holding his power
"from the people," each advance in his personal popularity
would set the stage for further weakening the legislative
power and reinforcing the executive, including Bonaparte's
hold on the Senate.

Once the constitution was in place, Bonaparte set out
to reorganize state administration, justice, finances, and the
police. There were of course many positions to distribute
in these ministries, which permitted him to name people
on whose loyalty he could rely.

A profound transformation in the political organization
of the country was made with the Law of 17 February 1800.
Although the old hierarchy of department, arrondissement,
and commune established by the Constituant Assembly was
kept in place, the method of selecting the representation of
each of these units was no longer entrusted to the electorate;
rather, representatives were appointed from Paris. Local
councils were henceforth filled by selections made by the
government from lists of names of local notables. The role
of the notables was reduced to preparing the local budget
(and even that had to be approved by the central government's representative) and to apportioning the burden of
direct state taxation among local taxpayers. The true masters
of local administration were thus the functionaries named
in Paris, beginning with the departmental prefects, who had
political as well as administrative functions: tending public
"spirit," "quickening" economic activity, overseeing military conscription. In sum, the principle of local administrative autonomy, established by the Revolution, disappeared.

The First Consul selected his prefects with extreme care
from lists made up by his two colleagues, as well as by
Talleyrand and Lucien Bonaparte, the latter often having

the last word. The most commonly selected candidates were former revolutionaries, now repentant and moderate. Then came former functionaries, a few generals, and a handful of representatives of the high nobility, who had rallied to the Revolution. Napoleonic centralization was in truth more far-reaching and efficient than that of the Old Regime. The monarchy had administered more than it governed; the Napoleonic regime governed and administered.

The reform law of 18 March 1800 brought French justice into harmony with the new principle of authority. The hierarchy introduced by the Constitution of the Year VIII predominated: the court of first instance was the justice of the peace; at the departmental level came criminal courts, assisted by grand juries. Beyond this, the work of the Revolution was significantly altered. The twenty-nine appellate courts, in their number, titles and powers, recalled the parlements of the Old Regime. Except for justices of the peace, no magistrate was elected. Appellate justices were named by the Senate, and all the others by the First Consul. Judges who handed down sentences could not be removed, but they depended on the government for their advancement. Finally, in each tribunal, in the place of a public prosecutor, a removable commissioner was appointed by Paris. His job was not only to present the state's case, but to keep an eye on his judicial colleagues.

In selecting judges, the government called not only on the magistrates of the Old Regime, but on those lawyers who had stood out in the Revolution, or for that matter on anyone known for his intellectual accomplishment. To extirpate brigandage, special courts were established. A February 1801 law authorized the government to set up special tribunals wherever it deemed them useful to mete out swift punishment for theft, violence, arson, counterfeiting, and certain cases of homicide. Composed of three judges, three other officers, and two citizens designated by the First Consul, they tried offenders without jury, and their findings stood without appeal.

Bonaparte expected efficient functioning of his ministry of police, which he had turned over to Fouché. But to prevent Fouché from becoming too powerful, Bonaparte gave him a rival in the Prefect of Police for Paris. In the departments, the general and special commissioners were not always responsible solely to Fouché. Finally, though nominally responsible to Fouché, the secret police had its own director in Desmarets. Lavalette, as director general of the post office, also performed very useful services for the First Consul by overseeing the mail of the diplomatic corps as well as anyone held in political suspicion.

The national gendarmerie, which the Revolution had created, was also reorganized. Separate from the police and justice ministries, it was fundamentally a military body, placed under the command of Moncey, and responsible for overseeing public order, especially in the countryside, and more especially where the draft was concerned. Moncey had his own espionage service and controlled secret funds for which he was accountable only to Bonaparte.

All these police and paramilitary bodies furnished the First Consul with reports that were compiled in a daily résumé, informing him of criminal activity, to be sure, but mostly on the state of public opinion.

On the morrow of the Brumaire coup, the French treasury was empty. To remedy this situation, Bonaparte took action in close collaboration with Gaudin, his minister of finance, Mollien, director of the Sinking Fund [Caisse d'amortissement] and Barbé-Marbois, director (later, in 1803, minister) of the treasury. Throughout almost the entire Year VIII, the most pressing financial problems were met with expedients and improvisations. Loans were made to the government by bankers and merchants, nationalized lands were sold, special securities were required of notaries, financial agents, and lawyers, and further efforts were made to extract money from the occupied countries (Holland, the Cisalpine Republic, Pedmont, Genoa). Only by the frankly brigand-like methods of the Directory could the government obtain an accurate audit of the state debt. A law of 21 March 1801, passed over the veto of the Tribunate, simply imposed an arbitrary reduction on the debt, from 110 to 37 million francs.

In addition, measures were taken to restore public confidence. One of the most popular was the Concordat of Interest paid on government bonds [the *rente*]. Passed on 11 April 1800, it declared that henceforth interest and government pensions would be paid on time and in hard money.

The policy originally envisioned by the Directory to improve the financial image of the government in the eyes of taxpayers was thus brought full course. The centralization of state financial administration was strengthened by the creation of the Office of Direct Taxation. Municipalities lost all autonomy in this domain. From the cantonal to the departmental level, the state installed a hierarchy of its agents to handle taxation. But to guarantee the honesty of its fiscal officials, the government had recourse to a practice of the Old Regime. Revenue agents were obliged to lend to the state over the course of any given year the amount they expected to collect in taxes in their area. Such a procedure obviously was intended to furnish the treasury with immediate means. The law of 29 November 1799 created, for this purpose, a sinking fund, subsidized by the security paid in by tax agents, which both diminished the state debt and maintained the level of the all-important state interest payments, about which Bonaparte, with his hand on the public pulse, never failed to be concerned.

The direct taxes created by the Directory furnished the state with two-thirds of its receipts, the remainder coming from customs, licensing, stamp, and tobacco taxes. To provide a good yield, the land tax required each commune to set up a careful land survey [cadastre], but the necessary law was not passed until 1807. Bonaparte never hid his preference for indirect taxes, but if he acted prudently here, it was because he feared causing public discontent. He waited until 1804 to introduce, timidly, a liquor tax and to establish the Office of Duties, which oversaw the collection of all indirect taxes.

For now, the financial situation improved; the budget of the Year X (1801–1802) was balanced at about 500 million . francs. With the return of war came a return of the deficit, but war again brought its own remedy, the exploitation of conquered lands.

On 13 February 1800, the Bank of France was created. It was obliged to make loans to the treasury to cover state expenses that were due before taxes could be collected. To this end, the government also had recourse to certain bankers who had financed the Brumaire coup. The bank was a private institution, created with 30 million francs in capital, in shares of 1,000 francs each. The government provided initial funding from the securities paid by state fiscal agents, the receipts of Paris tolls, and the state lottery. In exchange, the bank had to assure that state interest payments and pension obligations would be met, and make loans to the treasury against future tax income. Its second principal function was to rediscount commercial bills of exchange [*reescompte des effets de commerce*]. To accomplish this, the bank used monies from both the public fund and private investments it received. It is thus not an exaggeration to say that the bank's founders were able to use public monies for their own profit. The law of 18 April 1803, besides raising the Bank's capital to 45 million francs, granted it a monopoly on minting money. This law also definitively set in place the bank's administrative council, fifteen regents and three proctors elected by the 200 largest shareholders. The state did not control the operations of these regents, in whose hands it nonetheless deposited public funds. Not until 1806 would the council include three directors named by the government.

The financial reorganization was complete with the law of 7 Germinal XI (27 March 1803), which established the franc as the basic unit of currency. Bimetalism continued at a ratio of 15.5 between the value of gold and that of silver with the price of gold being set at 3.10 francs per gram. The franc was defined as the value of 5 grams of silver of .322 grams of gold, a value that stood until 1914.

In a very short time Bonaparte had managed to stabilize the Revolution, giving France the institutions that she had been waiting for since 1791 while preserving the preponderance of the revolutionary bourgeoisie. He imprinted on the consulate characteristics that the empire would accentuate: centralization, authoritarianism, and bureaucratic government. The Old Regime had made Frenchmen subjects; the Revolution made them citizens. The consulate reduced them to being objects of administration.

Domestic Pacification

Bonaparte would bring this off over a two-year period during which he alternately made concessions and inflicted repression, presenting himself as the defender of order against "brigandage" and "anarchy." Even before the promulgation of the constitution, the law on hostages had been retained and a preliminary armistice was signed with the Vendée insurgents (24 November 1799). On 28 December, they were given ten days to hand over their weapons and promised amnesty and the replacement of the old, hated clerical oath of the Revolution with a simple declaration of loyalty to the constitution. On 17 January 1800, a tough measure was taken against freedom of expression: sixty of seventy-three Paris newspapers were suppressed, and founding any new ones was prohibited throughout the country.

Yet domestic order was hard to achieve, for the political oppositions would not easily let themselves be disarmed. The fragility of Bonaparte's power appeared most clearly when he had to rejoin the army in Italy (May to July 1800). Only a victory against the foreign enemy assured him of victory over his enemies within France. Many of the men of Brumaire and the Ideologues bitterly reproached themselves for having pulled Bonaparte's chestnuts out of the fire at their own expense. They may have received titles, but power escaped them. At the very least they hoped to slow his ascendance or win some advantage over him. In this they could count on the support of certain members of the Bonaparte clan, notably on Lucien who had been poorly recompensed for his role on 19 Brumaire. In addition, the generals were becoming jealous. Moreau, Bernadotte, Brune, Lecourbe, and Jourdan resented suddenly finding themselves subordinate to Bonaparte. Nor were all these discontented ones missing the company of a Siéyès, a Barras, a Talleyrand, or a Fouché. Beginning in January 1800, the opposition showed itself in the Tribunate, where Benjamin Constant denounced the dangers of a regime of servitude and silence. But when Bonaparte got angry, his opponents backed down, for they had no popular support that could have made them dangerous.

Such was not the case with the royalist opposition that had reawakened in the west after the summer of 1799. Here again Bonaparte employed a dual policy. Brune and 50,000 men were sent to Brittany, while Paris used an Angevin priest named Bernier to carry on secret negotiations. The refractory clergy was unofficially tolerated. As a result, most Chouan chieftains, their cause appeased, surrendered their arms. On 3 March 1800, the list of émigrés was declared officially closed, but this did not disarm the royalist party. On Jersey, in Souabe and in Paris, royalist agents remained in correspondence with one another plotting insurrections in the west, the Midi, and in the capital, where demonstrations had taken place on the anniversary of the death of the king (21 January). Certain royalists, it is true, hoped that Bonaparte might open the way to a restoration. They even convinced the pretender to write twice to the First Consul, making him enticing offers for his assistance in bringing about such a project.

By the time the Italian campaign of the year 1800 opened, public opinion was again somewhat uncertain. All now depended on the outcome of the war. Bonaparte fully understood that any defeat would seriously endanger his power. In effect, he was condemned to be always victorious. The men of Brumaire were agitating again, and Madame de Staël hoped the First Consul would be beaten in Italy so that tyranny would be blocked from definitively installing itself in France. As it happened, the Battle of Marengo (officially reported in Paris as a resounding victory) provided Bonaparte with greater glory and popularity than he had previously enjoyed. When he returned to Paris, he was acclaimed even by the poorer sections of the city, that had, until then, proven somewhat indifferent, not to say hostile, because of the high price of bread. From this time to the end of the empire, the revolutionary quarters of Paris provided Napoleon with his most loyal supporters, a hard blow to Jacobinism, to be sure. Thus he could fairly reply to Louis XVIII (7 September 1800), "You must not hope for a return to France. You would have to march over a hundred thousand corpses."

On 29 October 1800, 52,000 names were struck from the official register of émigrés, and a number of ecclesiastics and nobles returned to France. Any of their lands that were not already nationalized were given back to them. A certain number even entered the administration and the army. Simultaneously, the order was given to finish once and for all with "brigandage" (that is, the royalist opposition) in the west. The army of Bernadotte put 250 Chouans to death.

At this time a certain group of men of Brumaire, mostly former Feuillants, (a moderate, mostly pro-monarchist faction/club, in opposition to the Mountain/Jacobins, 1790–1794) took it upon themselves to push Bonaparte to establish his own monarchy as a means of stabilizing the regime. He felt it was too early to cut himself off so completely from the republicans, however. But he did disavow his brother Lucien, who lost the Ministry of the Interior for having disseminated a pamphlet entitled "Parallel between Caesar, Cromwell, and Bonaparte." Lucien thus managed to award himself a republican testimonial on the cheap, while giving a warning to his brother.

One might well wonder if the four Jacobin plots that were denounced between August and October of 1800 did not contain some police perfidy to serve as a pretext for arresting republican leaders. The government used the royalist agitation to justify the repression of the Jacobins.

From Brittany, Cadoudal had dispatched several emissaries to Paris to carry out assassinations of certain people. On 24 December 1800, in the rue Saint-Nicaise, an infernal machine exploded just as the First Consul's carriage rolled by. He was not hurt, but twenty-six died. Fouché knew perfectly well that it was a royalist action, but Bonaparte accused the Jacobins, and Fouché went along with him. A certain number of the republicans were guillotined or shot, and 130 others were sentenced without trials to deportation to the Seychelles. Shortly after, the Chouan leaders, Saint-Réjean and Carbon, were arrested (and soon executed) for their roles in the rue Saint-Nicaise attempt. Nevertheless, Bonaparte enforced the measures against the Jacobins, for he wished to have done with an opposition that the coup of 18 Brumaire had not been able to quell and thereby prove to Europe that he was a defender of order. Cadoudal momentarily revived the royalist movement in Brittany, but the mobile columns sent from Paris destroyed him. At last Bonaparte understood that the royalist peril remained the most dangerous, and that to shatter the popular appeal of royalism, only a religious pacification would suffice.

In Italy and Egypt, Bonaparte readily grasped the full political and social importance of religion. Better than the anticlerical Ideologues who filled the major administrative posts of the state, he sensed that fine distinctions between the oath-taking and the refractory clergy meant little to the average Frenchman, who, encouraged by the religous reawakening taking place, yearned for a return to one rite and one clergy. For Napoleon, religion was a crucial element of social order, no more and no less. Any entente with Rome must bring a reinforcement of his own authority, if only because it would rally Catholics away from royalism and make of them what they had been under the monarchy: docile subjects.

Negotiations with the Catholic church opened after Marengo and ended on 16 July 1801. Bonaparte demanded that certain changes brought about by the Revolution be maintained: religious liberty, secularization of the state, and, especially, the definitive abolition of the clerical tax [the *dîme*] as well as the church's promise not to raise trouble over the sale of its nationalized lands. Pius VII also sanctioned the new ecclesiastical division of France into 60 dioceses (for 102 departments). The pope could not obtain from the French government that Catholicism be recognized as the religion of state (though he had gotten as much in the concordat he had signed with the Italian Republic, of which Bonaparte was president, but in Italy, Napoleon had not faced a fiercely secular Ideologue opposition.) The church did make some gains: Catholicism was proclaimed "the religion of the majority of Frenchmen," and the government undertook to pay "a decent salary" to bishops and diocesan clergy. As the king had done before 1789, the First Consul would name bishops, the pope retaining only the right to confer on them canonical investiture. Before they could take up their duties, bishops and priests had to swear to obey the constitution, to enter into "no association contrary to public tranquility," and to denounce any enterprise they knew of which was "prejudicial to the State." Bishops in short now became "prefects in violet."

The great majority of the populace applauded the concordat, but hostility to it was lively in the two legislative houses and in the army, where there was much opposition to "the clerical crew." To appease antireligious sentiment and turn back dissent in the Tribunate, Bonaparte tacked onto the concordat certain Organic Articles, without the pope's agreement, which permitted the French government to increase its hold over the Catholic church. These articles, of gallican inspiration, reduced to a minimum the French clergy's obedience to pontifical authority. Government authorization was needed for any papal bull or conciliar act to be published in France, as well as for the convocation of any assembly of French bishops. The articles also required a civil ceremony before the religious rite in marriage, and the teaching of the gallican Declaration of 1682 was mandated in French seminaries. Finally, to underscore that Catholicism had not become the religion of state again, Protestant denominations were officially recognized and organized along the same lines as those laid down for the Roman church. Pastors now received a state salary.

One single bill, composed of the concordat and the Organic Articles, was passed on 8 April 1802. Unquestionably it was a defeat for the anticlerical Ideologues. By giving Bonaparte the credit for "restoring the altars," it further increased his popularity, and by subjecting the church to the state, it contributed palpably to his authority.

6. International Pacification (1800–1802)

As French peace offers to England and Austria went without response, it became necessary to fight. A reserve army of 60,000 men was called up and placed under Bonaparte's personal command, but only 49,000 of the conscripts actually reported for duty. Care had been taken to demobilize older units to make room for new ones, but from the outset Bonaparte found himself confronted with every general's scourge: desertion. Before leaving on campaign (April 1800), he inaugurated a habit that he would use to the end: publishing a proclamation to the French nation in which he assured everyone that he was making war only to win a definitive peace.

The reserve army held itself in readiness to march into Switzerland, there to strike either at Germany (to support Moreau) or at Italy (to support Masséna and Suchet). Austrian successes in the peninsula decided the matter: Bonaparte struck at Italy. To gain the element of surprise, he marched his poorly equipped troops over the Alpine pass of Grand Saint-Bernard (14 to 15 May 1800). Turning the Austrian right, he entered Milan on 2 June. An inadequate or faulty corps of scouts (such mistakes would happen again) led Bonaparte to disperse his troops to the southwest in single divisions, each without enough artillery. He himself encountered the numerically superior troops of General Mélas on the plain of Marengo (14 June). Early in the engagement, Mélas believed himself victorious and dispatched bulletins to that effect. When Mélas's news reached Paris, Bonaparte's opposition felt its time had finally come. But by the evening of the 14th, the arrival of fresh French reinforcements under Desaix turned the tide and gave victory to Bonaparte. Marengo was thus a kind of reverse Waterloo fifteen years earlier, though it was bought at the high price of Desaix's death on the field. The announcement in the *Army Bulletin* of 15 June, describing Bonaparte as infallible and invincible, was a tissue of lies and half-truths. The armistice enabled the French to reoccupy Piedmont and restore the Cisalpine and Ligurian republics.

But it was in Germany, much to Bonaparte's distaste, that the issue was decided. Moreau had already invaded Bavaria and taken Munich. He now crushed the Archduke John at Hohenlinden on 3 December and opened the road to Vienna, obliging Austria to sue for peace. A treaty was signed at Lunéville on 9 February 1801. The French hold on Belgium and the left bank of the Rhine was recognized. In addition, her influence in Germany was considerably strengthened by the compensations in right-bank lands granted to those lay princes of the left bank who had been expropriated (and who tended to favor French interests). Austria further recognized the Batavian and Helvetic Republics, vassals of France. In Italy, she kept Venice, but was obliged to recognize the Cisalpine and Ligurian republics, which were bases of French hegemony in the northern peninsula. Austria was also obliged to accept the dethroning of the Habsburg prince, Ferdinand, in Tuscany, whose crown was given to the duke of Parma, a relation of the Spanish sovereigns who were allies of France. (Spain, in turn, ceded Louisiana to France.) Bonaparte soon had himself elected president of the Cisalpine Republic (25 January 1802). This extension of his power could only render the Peace of Lunéville the more precarious.

When peace was signed with Russia on 8 October 1801, France had no remaining adversary on the Continent. Her natural frontiers were now attained and assured, and the nation finally had the victorious peace she had hoped for. However, there remained the matter of England. Having taken rather authoritarian steps to block the Continent to French trade, England had angered some of her former allies and now saw allied against her a League of Neutrals, led by Tsar Paul I, which included Sweden, Denmark, and Prussia as well as Russia. Britain thus ran the risk of losing two important markets: Germany and the Baltic countries. Pitt resigned in February, 1801, thereby removing one of the major obstacles to peace. Negotiations opened and would last a year.

England had occupied Malta on 25 September 1800. With the capitulation of the French army in Egypt (April 1801) and a peace signed with Turkey (October 1801), she was mistress of the Mediterranean and therefore could take a tougher posture in the talks. But when Bonaparte assembled troops and ships along the Channel, the English public panicked, though perhaps less in anxiety about a possible invasion than in concern over a serious economic crisis that brought rising bread prices and a falling rate of exchange. Businessmen, hoping that it would favor an economic recovery, pushed their government to peace. Preceded by preliminaries in London (October 1801), the peace was finally signed at Amiens on 25 March 1802.

By this treaty, France recovered the Antilles and its settlements in India. England recovered its Latin American port, Trinity, and Ceylon, which were taken away from Spain and Holland, allies of France. England promised to evacuate Egypt and to return Malta to the Knights of Malta.

Certain key questions were avoided, however: nothing was said about commercial relations between France and England, and London did not expressly recognize either French natural frontiers or its vassal states.

Nonetheless, for the first time in ten years Europe was at peace. In France, the credit for this redounded entirely to Bonaparte. Nobody stopped to consider that the treaties contained equivocations which rendered them dangerously fragile. Eight weeks after Amiens, Bonaparte called up 60,000 new conscripts.

7. Citizen Bonaparte Becomes Napoleon Bonaparte

The signing of the peace, along with the silence imposed on the domestic oppositions and the resolution of the religious question, heightened the First Consul's prestige. It now remained only for him to succeed where Louis XVI and the Revolution had failed: to solve the twin problems of food distribution and unemployment that had caused so many riots in the past and shaken so many governments. They were the problems that now held his attention.

Vanquishing the Economic Crisis

From spring to summer of 1801, the price of bread reached alarming levels, while unemployment appeared in all the industrial centers of France. Public morale sharply declined as looting increased in the provinces. Bonaparte put into practice the advice he had given Melzi, vice-president of the Italian Republic: make it a point that the price of wheat be one issue on which the government "should always favor the proletariat against property owners." He took steps to make bread cheap, particularly in Paris, including regulating bakeries, purchasing additional shipments of wheat in Holland and Italy, and severely punishing hoarders.

In the fight against unemployment, he further expanded the public works projects that had been begun after Marengo, including cutting a route through Simplon and Mont-Cenis in the Alps, as well as the Saint-Quentin canal. He launched a major program of embellishments of the city of Paris. By the end of 1802, the food crisis was over and unemployment was clearly falling—developments that made a greater impression on the public than did the signing of Amiens.

Repressing the Republican Opposition
Although the republicans fell quiet after Marengo, they had no intention of relinquishing their political role. The left opposition soon made itself felt in the legislative assemblies. The Tribunate caused problems over the government's intention to create special courts, and it vigorously criticized Bonaparte's project of a new civil code. Cleverly, Bonaparte fought the assemblies by making it seem as though the antiparliamentary sentiment was deeply anchored in public opinion. The Tribunate was purged by the Senate, which, instead of designating candidates to that body by drawing lots, selected out all rebellious elements (for example, Benjamin Constant and Daunou). Soon afterward, using the same device, the Legislative Body was stripped of its less docile members. On 1 April 1802, the Tribunate was divided into three distinct sections, each deliberating in exclusion from the others. Madame de Staël, whose salon served as the unofficial headquarters of the Ideologues, was "invited" to leave Paris. Without popular support to begin with, the

parliamentary opposition now ceased altogether to be a serious danger to Bonaparte.

Such was not the case with the opposition in the army. The jealousy felt by many generals toward their uniquely successful colleague did not diminish. Moreover, a number of the more Jacobin-leaning generals were alarmed at the concessions being made to the right-wing enemies of the Revolution. From April to June 1802, no fewer than four military conspiracies were uncovered aimed either at assassinating the First Consul or at overthrowing him. Bernadotte, Augereau, MacDonald, Masséna, Lecourbe, and others were implicated, though it must be said that they plotted like amateurs. Bonaparte easily confuted their plans. He declared to the Council of State: "A military regime will never work in France. . . . I don't hesitate to say that first and foremost, France incontestably belongs to a civil government." Dismissals were handed out to some generals (Lecourbe), whereas others were placed on the inactive list (MacDonald), and still others were sent off on distant diplomatic missions (Brune and Lannes), or compelled to take vacations (Bernadotte was sent to the seaside town of Plombières). After this, the remaining malcontents all fell into line.

The Consulate for Life

Since Marengo, and more especially since the Peace of Amiens, what could only be called a Bonapartist opinion undoubtedly prevailed both among the notables and the general population. In this group, a particular current of thought held that only some variety of neo-monarchist institution could consolidate the First Consul's power. Bonaparte himself was only too pleased to rely on and cultivate such opinion. Heretofore he had talked about consolidating his political edifice through the creation of what he called "blocks of granite" amidst the innumerable "grains of sand" that constituted French society. That is to say, he hoped to assure popular obedience by forming intermediary elite bodies between the nation and the citizenry.

To assure the future of the consulate, he wished to form the minds of young Frenchmen at the earliest possible age. Such was the object of the law of 1 May 1802, which established high schools [lycées] and placed all secondary education under state control. To Bonaparte's way of thinking, lycées would form the sons of the notables to benefit the state, not least through the training of future officers, functionaries, and business leaders. The schools were to receive 6,400 scholarships, of which 2,400 were earmarked for the sons of high-level government functionaries and military officers. The poor would receive none, though the lower and middle bourgeoisie would receive some help in nudging their sons up the social ladder. Latin and mathematics were the principal subjects of study, though religious education was not neglected. The discipline at the lycées was entirely military: uniforms were worn, drumbeats regulated the school day, and so forth. The success of the schools was less rapid than Bonaparte hoped for, however, for the lycées had competitors in the private schools. In any case, the lycées clearly reveal Bonaparte's desire to form the minds of the classes, which he felt constituted the state's "armor."

A law of 18 May 1802 founded the Legion of Honor, demonstrating Bonaparte's intention to adapt to the new regime a custom that had proven itself under the kings. In his mind, the legion would weave strong personal bonds between its members and the head of state who conferred the honor. Its immediate purpose was to reward achievement, but ultimately the legion was intended to contribute to the reconstruction of an elite, which France certainly needed. It would be a republican aristocracy, open to everyone on the basis of merit and services rendered to the state. Legionnaires were required to take a special oath to defend the state and French society, and to "combat any enterprise tending to re-establish the feudal order and its [noble] titles." Despite this precaution, however, the monarchical character of the new institution provoked considerable opposition in the legislative assemblies.

On 6 May, 1802, after it had ratified the Peace of Amiens, the Tribunate expressed the wish that Bonaparte be offered a "dazzling token of the nation's gratitude." The Senate limited itself to offering "Napoleon Bonaparte" a ten-year renewal of his term of consul. (This was the first time his first name appeared in an official act.) Vexed at this paltry offer, Bonaparte made known to the Senate that he would not accept such powers except from the people. This amounted to calling for a plebiscite, which took place soon after, though not on the issue of a ten-year renewal but rather on the question, "Should Napoleon Bonaparte be named consul for life?" On August 2, the Senate proclaimed the results: 8,394 opposed (six times as many as in 1799; half the no votes came from the army), and 3,508,895 in favor (500,000 more than in 1800; however, the left bank of the Rhine was now part of France).

The Senatorial declaration [sénatus-consulte] of 4 August 1802, wrongly known as the Constitution of the Year X, in effect merely changed the consulate of the Year VIII into a life consulate. The First Consul received the right to name his successor as well as his two co-consuls, the right to sign peace treaties without legislative approval, and the right of pardon. A personal council of ten members (whom the First Consul named) was created to assist Bonaparte, thus reducing the Council of State to a merely juridical body. The Senate saw its authority increased; it could now "complete and interpret the constitution" with "organic decrees" [*sénatus-consulte*], as well as dissolve the legislative assemblies and overturn judgments handed down by the courts. On the other hand, the Senate paid for such gains by becoming further domesticated by the First Consul, who could now name forty senators from the lists provided him by the electoral colleges. To compensate the more docile senators, a *sénatorerie* was created in each administrative district of France, itself based on the territorial jurisdiction of a Court of Appeals. Each *sénatorerie* was granted by the First Consul for life and consisted of a sumptuous residence and certain revenues drawn from the nationalized lands valued at 20,000 to 25,000 francs a year. As for the Legislative Body, it ceased holding regular sessions, whereas the Tribunate was reduced to a rump of fifty members.

The so-called Constitution of the Year X created in the nation one of the "blocks of granite" on which the new society would stand. Local lists of "trusted" candidates were now replaced by regular electoral colleges. Cantonal assemblies, made up of all citizens, elected municipal councils and justices of the peace from official lists of 100 candidates. From other lists (of more than 600 names), they designated members of arrondissement and departmental electoral colleges, who were named for life. As for filling places in arrondissement and general councils, and in the legislative assemblies and the Senate, the electoral colleges would present the names of two candidates to the Senate, which would select the appointee. Universal suffrage henceforth played into the hands of the wealthiest, for the amount of tax paid was easily the largest factor in conferring the franchise. The electoral colleges were dominated by social groups whose wealth, either wholly or in large measure, stemmed from the land. This elite thus brought together the former landowners of the Old Regime with the new landowners—both loyal groups because of their role as proprietors.

By consolidating his power, Napoleon could force the legislature to pass the French Civil Code, promulgated on 21 March 1804. He was personally interested in the project because of his knowledge of law. Better than anything else, the Civil Code symbolizes the Napoleonic stabilization of the Revolution. It would be pointless to deny the reactionary character of certain elements of the code stemming from Roman law or ancient custom; the power of a husband over his wife or of a father over his children, for example; but it is no less true that everything that seemed to contemporaries to embody revolutionary conquests also found a place in the code, beginning with the laicization of law through the exclusion of religion in civil matters (notably, marriage). Moreover, the code solemnly confirmed the great principles of the Declaration of the Rights of Man: personal freedom, equality among citizens, suppression of privileges attached to title or social class, the free disposition and inviolability of property, equal inheritance, the binding power of contracts freely arrived at, and so forth. The code was the Revolution made law, supported by the full authority of social conservatism. Confirming the abolition of stratification based on juridical privilege, it replaced it with the economic power of wealth, theoretically open to everyone. The code placed salaried income juridically below proprietary wealth. Article 1781, for example, stipulated that in matters of public trust, "an owner is to be believed [over a worker] at his word." Laws passed in April and December 1803 renewed the prohibition of unions and strikes, but required salaried employees to carry a license [*livret*] that effectively put them under state surveillance.

Appearing as a compromise between the old and the new regimes, the Civil Code confirmed the evolution of French society since 1789 by establishing the triumph of the principles of authority and social conservation. Ironically this all took place at just the same time as a debate over the transformation of the consulate into a hereditary monarchy.

8. Napoleon Bonaparte Becomes Napoleon the First

The Peace of Amiens was surely one of Bonaparte's greatest successes, contributing decisively to the consolidation of his prestige, but because he broke with the royalists, and they resumed their plots against the regime, his power was transformed into a hereditary monarchy.

The Beginnings of the Continental System
Napoleon himself first used the phrase "continental system" to define the complex politics of exclusion that he inaugurated in Europe. From the outset he felt that the tranquility of France could not be assured unless the antagonism between the Revolution and the Old Regime in Europe disappeared. To this end, although he hoped that every nation

would transform its institutions and social conventions in conformity with the French model, Napoleon sought to set up a *cordon sanitaire* of allied regimes separating France from the other great powers of the continent. Fundamentally, however, the continental system was an economic policy. A good mercantilist, Bonaparte believed that French prosperity demanded a positive balance of payments. This, in turn, required the re-establishment of the colonial empire and its commerce in primary goods (a heritage of the Old Regime) and the erection of high tariffs to protect French industry against foreign competition while ensuring open markets for French goods (a heritage of the Directory).

In the name of French security, Bonaparte refused to withdraw his troops from Holland, and forbade the Dutch to contract any offensive or defensive alliances.

In Germany, the indemnification of the dispossessed lay princes on the left bank of the Rhine was used to justify the increase of French influence. A Franco-Russian proposal was approved by the imperial Diet on 25 February 1803. The lay states allied with France—Prussia, Bavaria, Wurtemburg, and Baden—were compensated at the expense of the ecclesiastical principalities and the free cities far beyond any losses they had sustained. The total number of German state was reduced by half; only one ecclesiastical elector was maintained (the archbishop of Mainz, now translated to Ratisbon). Only six of fifty-one free cities remained. Bonaparte thus created a "middle size" power in Germany, consisting of Bavaria, Baden, and Wurtemburg, which, if they united could contain Prussia and Austria, but were nevertheless not strong enough among themselves to forego French support.

In Switzerland, Bonaparte implemented an Act of Mediation (18 February 1803), which created the Helvetic Confederation of nineteen cantons, equal before the law, each with its own institutions and (in most cases) franchises. The new constitution was placed under the protection of the French First Consul, who, in addition, directed Swiss foreign policy. The confederation had to sign with France a defenive alliance for fifty years.

In Italy, Bonaparte evacuated several Neapolitan ports and the Papal States (15 September 1802), but Piedmont was annexed to France. In January 1802, the Cisalpine Republic had become the Italian Republic under the presidency of Bonaparte. He endowed it with a constitution modeled on that of the Year VIII, except for universal suffrage, and the concordat he signed on its behalf recognized Catholicism as the religion of state. The Ligurian Republic meanwhile saw itself forced to accept a constitution that reduced it to a protectorate with a permanent French military presence. Thanks to Bonaparte, Louis of Bourbon, son-in-law of the king of Spain, took possession of Tuscany, now the kingdom of Etruria. In return he ceded the island of Elba to France (1802) and agreed to maintain a French garrison. On the death of the duke of Parma, his state was occupied and made into an autonomous territory under a French commissioner (October 1802).

Buffer states were obligated to billet French troops, and some were even required to supply contingents for France. Thus, for example, in 1802 Switzerland was "taxed" to remit 16,000 men. In the same year, conscription was levied on the Italian Republic to provide 24,000 recruits. Becoming satellites of France was rarely to the taste of the local patriots.

Meanwhile the economic dispositions of the continental system, aimed at instituting French hegemony, were laid in place throughout Europe. Bonaparte wanted to restore to France its monopoly on commerce in exotic goods. After the signing of the Peace of Amiens, France found itself at the head of a considerably greater colonial empire than she had held in 1789—including various English colonies, Louisiana (from Spain), and, thanks to Toussaint l'Ouverture, the eastern part of Santo Domingo. On a landscape ravaged by war and social convulsion, Bonaparte tried to rebuild the administrative institutions of the Old Regime. This included reinstituting slavery (the law of 17 May 1802), although doing so provoked a revolt and, ultimately, cost him Santo Domingo. In the economic arena, Bonaparte returned to the system of the Colonial Pact; colonial goods that originated in England thus remained prohibited in France. Finally, he envisaged the creation of a vast American empire, extending from Guyana to Louisiana. Unfortunately, his actual attempts at achieving this, including repressive military expeditions in Santo Domingo and Guadaloupe, angered both the United States and England. In April 1803, with war threatening, Bonaparte believed that Louisiana would certainly be lost, so he sold it to the United States.

The Near East, whence came Macedonian and Smyrnian cotton, constituted yet another source of colonial products. The treaty signed in 1802 with the Turkish empire revived the era of Turkish capitulationism and reopened the Black Sea to French commerce. By this arrangement, France could count on receiving eastern cotton via the Balkans until 1815. She also entered into accords with the Barbary Coast states to secure freedom of navigation and improve French commerce.

In sum, France placed the import of goods produced abroad under a quasiprohibition. Heeding French manufacturers, Bonaparte refused to renew the Franco-British treaty of commerce of 1786 or to abolish the law of 10 Brumaire, Year V, proscribing the importation of all foreign-made goods. Instead, the First Consul did what was in his power both to ensure French industry a monopoly on the internal market and to secure for it markets on the Continent: he enforced the treaties signed during the Revolution with various German states and the Cisalpine Republic that accorded preference (without reciprocity) to French products, while imposing similar regimes on Portugal and Turkey.

The Resumption of the War

French encroachments in Europe alarmed Austria, whose influence redounded on Germany. They also alarmed Russia, who saw in the Franco-Turkish rapprochement an obstacle to its ambitions, and, above all, England, who was unhappy with French annexations in Italy. British ire focused more intensely on French tariff policy, on French naval and commercial activity in the Mediterranean, and on certain specific French initiatives, including Sébastiani's missions to Egypt and Syria, Baudin's to Australia, and Cavaignac's to Muscat. Finally, the nomination of Decaen as capitain general of French economic penetration in India aroused concern that France might well be preparing a military strike on Egypt or India. Faced with what she took to be serious provocations, England drew closer to the Russian empire.

The rupture, when it came, was thus London's doing. The British refused to evacuate Malta, as required by the

Treaty of Amiens. Instead, on 15 March 1803, His Majesty's government demanded retention of the island in exchange for British recognition of French conquests. On 26 April, confident of the tsar's backing, the British confronted France with an ultimatum. A fortnight later, they withdrew their ambassador from Paris, and on 16 May, their navy seized all French and Dutch ships standing at anchor in British ports. On the 23d of that month they formally declared war on France.

Until England could resurrect the continental coalition (July 1805), the two adversaries were engaged mainly in a fierce economic war. To unsettle British public opinion, Bonaparte assembled 150,000 men and 1,200 ships on the French edge of the English Channel. But calling up 60,000 men from the eligible names of the Year XII (1803–1804) caused problems, especially in the maritime regions of France, which suffered directly from the economic conflict with England. The British navy carried out an all but fatal war on French shipping, and victoriously attacked French colonies in the Antilles and Guyana. To combat British contraband, the French first occupied Flessigen and Dutch Brabant, then (June 1803) British Hanover. Soon after, consular decrees closed all French and German ports to English (and British colonial) merchandise. Even neutral cargoes could be admitted only if ship captains could produce a certificate attesting to the non-English origin of their goods. To close off the western Mediterranean littoral to English commerce, General Gouvion-Saint-Cyr was ordered to occupy Otranto, Brindisi, and Taranto. All British goods found in the Italian Republic were seized. And finally, by intensive diplomatic pressure, Bonaparte imposed his anti-British trade policy on Holland, Spain, and Portugal.

The Anglo-Royalist Conspiracy of the Year XI (1803)

While awaiting its chance to march on France with coalition armies, England lent its support to French royalists who wished to bring down the First Consul. In August 1803, a British ship disembarked the royalist agent and leader Cadoudal in Normandy as royalist bands recommenced roving about the western departments of France. Cadoudal had accomplices in the royal entourage of the count d'Artois, the duke de Berry, and the prince de Condé. He was also able to win over General Pichegru to his cause, though he failed to move General Moreau. In Paris itself, Cadoudal was able to set up a group of shock troops sufficient to stand up to the consular guard. In January 1804, he was formally joined by Polignac and Pichegru, but the plot was soon discovered. Moreau was banished (though he had stayed aloof from the royalists), and Pichegru was found strangled in his prison cell. Cadoudal himself was executed together with a dozen of his accomplices. Finally, during the night of 14–15 March 1804, the son of the prince de Condé, the duc d'Enghien was kidnapped. Hurriedly arraigned at the Vincennes fortress, d'Enghien was summarily judged and, a week later, shot as an émigré hired by the foreigner to invade France. An "abyss of blood" now separated Bonaparte forever from the Bourbons. The First Consul did not flinch, however. Until his own death (in 1821), he stalwartly claimed sole responsibility for the crime against d'Enghien.

The Establishment of the Empire (1804)

The Anglo-royalist conspiracy raised considerable public emotion and reinforced in the hearts of the men of Brumaire the sort of neo-monarchist sentiment that Champagny had defined as early as 1801: "We need a king who is king because I am a property holder, whose crown ensures that I am master of my property; we need therefore to be done with the Revolution, yet to have a king created by the Revolution, holding his rights from our own." In short, a monarch was devoutly desired by many as a consolidation of the Revolution's work, and the monarchy had to be hereditary to protect it against conspirators. When Cambacérès put the question of heredity before the Council of State, there were only seven noes out of twenty-seven votes. On 30 April 1804, a former convention member and regicide (who, on learning of the death of the duke d'Enghien, had said, "I am enchanted; Bonaparte has thus made himself a part of the Convention") proposed that the First Consul be declared emperor of the Republic, with the imperial title becoming heredity in his family. Only Carnot opposed this proposal, which was transmitted to the Senate.

This body drew up the *sénatus-consulte* of 25 Floréal, Year XII (18 May 1804), which has ever since been known incorrectly as the Constitution of the Year XII. "The government of the Republic is entrusted to an emperor who will take the title of emperor of the French. . . . Napoleon Bonaparte, presently First Consul of the Republic, is emperor of the French." The title of emperor thus avoided the sensitive title of king, difficult for anyone to carry after ten years of revolution. Other articles regulated the order of succession and outlined the creation of a new aristocracy by establishing six grand dignitaries, six grand officers of the crown, and sundry other official titles, whose number would include the marshals of the empire, to be named later. Napoleon held the right to name unlimited numbers of senators. Article 53 required that he take an oath "to maintain the integrity of the territory of the Republic, to respect and to make respected the laws of the concordat and the liberty of religion . . . , the equality of rights, political and civil liberty, the irrevocability of the sale of national lands." Thus the empire was established as a limited monarchy according to certain principles and interests of 1789. The ensuing plebiscite focused, not on the question of the imperial title itself, but on the matter of heredity. The results, 2,579 no votes versus 3,572,329 yes votes, solidly established the new regime as legitimate in popular opinion.

Yet the anointing desired by Napoleon had another purpose entirely—to base his crown on divine right. To be anointed by the pope himself moreover, was to one-up the Bourbons. On 2 December 1804, in Notre Dame Cathedral, a triple ceremony was held: the anointing of the monarch according to the traditional rites that made Napoleon "the blessed of the Lord," the self-coronation of Napoleon, and the swearing of the oath, after which Pius VII retired so as not to have to hear the emperor promise to respect the Organic Articles.

According to the *sénatus-consulte*, Napoleon was emperor of the French "by the grace of God and the constitutions of the Republic." The formula, "by the constitutions of the Republic," appeared for the last time in a decree of 28 May 1807. It was not until 1 January 1809 that the phrase, "French Empire" replaced that of "French Republic, Napoleon emperor" on the coins.

On 9 March 1805, the Italian Senate, convened in Paris, granted Napoleon the title of king of Italy; on the 26th, in the cathedral of Milan, he received the new crown, this time not sanctioned by any popular plebiscite. Napoleon thus turned his back on the revolutionary theory of a contract with the people.

CHAPTER 3

The Imperial Conquests (1804–1809)

*N*apoleon was torn three ways in his foreign policy: to respect his coronation oath concerning the integrity of the Republic, to bring home victory over England, and to put the continental system into effect. To this list one must add the obligations Napoleon undertook in becoming king of Italy, mediator of the Swiss Confederation, and, after 1806, protector of the Confederation of the Rhine. It is likely that if England had remained neutral, he would have succeeded in extending the continental system over all of Europe. As it was, however, the exigencies of all-out war led to the continental blockade and to placing members of the Bonaparte family on various thrones of Europe to ensure the success of the continental system. When the Spanish people rejected a "napoleonide" king, they too were added to the list of French enemies. In its purely economic aspects, the continental system tended to impel Napoleon to consider the states of Europe as so many colonies of the French Empire. Yet, on the other hand, the war with England obliged him to treat them as allies, on an equal footing with

France. Because he pursued contradictory objectives at the same time, any unitary explanation of Napoleonic foreign policy is difficult. Therefore the most divergent interpretations of First Empire diplomacy, each containing its own part of truth arise.

After the First Consul drew his sword on 20 May 1803, as emperor he could not sheathe it, constrained and obliged as he was to wage war until his abdication on 4 April 1814. Hostilities would then recommence on 13 May 1815, ceasing definitively only after Waterloo, on 22 June. Napoleon would pass his entire reign at war.

1. Napoleon at War: Tradition and Innovation

The emperor did not innovate in methods of recruitment. In an era when war was made mainly with masses of men, Napoleon filled his armies using the conscription system of 1798. That system nominally called to the colors all Frenchmen between the ages of twenty and twenty-five, though the law operated with numerous exceptions. In fact, the imperial army would become increasingly less French as its ranks were swelled by recruits from newly annexed departments. It is difficult to cite accurately the numbers mobilized. The only exact figures we possess refer to the units placed directly at the government's disposition. The total of the empire's levies was 2,100,000 men, to which must be added 185,000 called during the period 1801–1804, and 170,000 called up in earlier years. But these figures do not take into account either voluntary enrollments or the wounded who were demobilized, either those who went into retirement or those killed under fire or by sickness. Nor does it include deserters.

Taking the army of 1813 (900,000 conscripts) as an example, the heaviest levies took place in 1808 and 1812: 240,000 and 257,000, respectively. These numbers are lower than those of the last year of the Directory (412,000 men, called from only ninety-eight departments). In 1809, the year of the Battle of Wagram, only 76,000 conscripts were called, and from October 1809 to December 1810, none were called up. In relation to the population of the empire, these are very low figures. Even the maximum number, attained in 1813, represented only 2.85 percent, a percentage much smaller than in 1794 (4.17 percent), which had been called within the smaller limits of the old kingdom. From 1800 to 1814, 5.77 percent of the male population of the empire was conscripted. In short, and contrary to received wisdom, *"la grande nation"* was not the "nation armed." (A telling comparison: In 1914 France mobilized, in fifty-two months of war, one-fifth of its entire male population.) Although after 1807, the empire had recourse to anticipatory levies (except in 1811 and 1812), and although after 1808, certain numbers of previously unmobilized men from earlier years were called up, never—not even in 1813— was an entire age group incorporated whole into the army. The very heaviest levies affected at most 53.32 percent, a far cry from the 80 percent of certain years during the Great War.

Military conscription nevertheless encountered vigorous resistance from the people. In practice, the system passed over the clergy and the well-to-do, for after 1802, paid replacements were permitted. Moreover, one could legally escape one's military obligation by marrying, which led to a kind of race to the altar (the marriage rate rose from 7.9 percent at the end of the Old Regime to 12.9 percent in 1813, the highest recorded in French history). Besides marriage, two other means of escaping service became popular: draft dodging and desertion. During the empire, the flight from conscription was lower than during the consulate: 13 percent draft dodging in the Years IX and X compared to 1.6 percent in 1806. The percentage of deserters seems to have fallen even lower, but over the years of the empire accumulated desertions showed up as numerous gaps in the ranks by 1814.

Hostility to a regime is not necessarily the only motive for avoiding conscription, yet once one has evaded the draft, one usually becomes an opponent of the government that has labeled one an outlaw. There are some striking coincidences: the zones of high rates of refusal to serve included the new departments, except for the left bank of the Rhine, Corsica, and those maritime provinces adversely affected by the English blockade. In general, the strongholds of draft dodgers were where royalist sentiment was rife. As levies occurred more frequently, taking greater numbers of men facing diminishing prospects of demobilization at the end of their five-year term, and as wars became more murderous, military service grew increasingly unpopular. "Down with conscription!" was a cry as oft heard in 1814 as "down with high taxes!"

Certainly Napoleon did not overlook soliciting assistance from his satellite states, including even his occasional allies, Prussia and Austria. After Austerlitz, and especially after Tilset, whole armies were furnished by foreign countries, marching under their own banners in the imperial army. The Cisalpine Republic, now the Kingdom of Italy, provided 218,000 men, while the Kingdom of Naples, under Joseph Bonaparte, later under Marshal Murat, furnished

60,000. Spain (under Joseph) was required to supply a permanent contingent of 15,000 men; the Confederation of the Rhine, 60,000 (later doubled); Switzerland, 10,000; Holland (under King Louis Bonaparte), 25,000 (later 36,000). Marshal Junot conscripted Portuguese troops, and eventually even Poland contributed manpower.

As for instruction, Napoleon adhered loyally to the system of veterans teaching recruits, the teachers including many troops of the Revolution or even of the old royal army (which accounted for 170,000 men as late as 1803). Unfortunately, however, only in the long, lingering months of the encampment at Boulogne did fresh recruits ever actually receive a solid instruction before being sent under fire. As the number of veterans shrank and the number of recruits grew, the quality of Napoleonic soldiery left much to be desired. After 1809, this dearth of instruction was turning out troops that were inept in manoeuvres and less than dependable in combat. Improvised as a combatant, the Napoleonic soldier remained undisciplined, but then his emperor really asked only one thing of him: obedience under fire.

Nor was Napoleon an innovator in armaments. His weapons of choice remained the 1777 rifle and the Gribeauval cannon of 1774. Napoleon declined to pick up the breech-loading rifle of the arms manufacturer Pauly, just as he ignored the steam engine for navigation and the hot-air balloon for reconnaissance. And, until Waterloo, it was the English, not the French, who used shrapnel (for the first time in the Spanish campaign of 1808). Nevertheless, artillery was by and large the object of Napoleon's greatest attentions. He would say, "the fewer good troops are, the more they need artillery." Thus, little by little, he piled the cannon onto men, as French fire power increasingly had to compensate for inferior manoeuverability. As time passed, however, and war materiel was consumed, the quality of armaments grew steadily poorer.

As in preceding epochs, war was improvised. With his men's uniforms in tatters (peasant clogs [*sabots*] often replaced leather-soled shoes) the Napoleonic army sometimes resembled a band of beggars. After a victory, the soldiery would complete its material needs from the equipment of the foe. Provisioning functioned poorly despite the creation of baggage trains in 1807. Private suppliers were still needed for munitions, materiel, foodstuffs, and transport. The soldier was asked to live off the land, resulting often in his transformation into a marauder. Pay was irregularly distributed, and, even then, often came from exactions imposed on the defeated enemy. In 1806, the creation of the post of Intendant General, awarded to one of the empire's leading civil servants (Daru), improved these areas little. Nor was the army's health service any better organized. Despite the dedication of its chief, Larrey, the health service could not reduce the frighteningly high rates of mortality among the wounded and the sick.

Where Napoleon did innovate was, first, in the general organization of the army. After 1804, he began regrouping the too-numerous divisions of the Camp at Boulogne into army corps, each containing two or three infantry divisions, a light cavalry brigade and artillery, and outfitted with its own intelligence and service units as well as a full-sized general staff. He also set up a general reserve of cavalry (under the command of Murat) and of artillery. The Imperial Guard, which finally enlisted 90,000 men, functioned as a reserve force whose commitment in battle often decided the contest in Napoleon's favor. Yet perhaps because he had read too much Guibert and was himself a confirmed believer in a war of movement, Bonaparte neglected fortifications, an error for which France would pay dearly in 1814.

Napoleon's military genius displayed itself in the way he deployed army corps to embrace an entire theater of operations, in his ability to disconcert the enemy with feints, and in his talent for constraining him to battle on terrain of the emperor's choosing and cutting off the routes of retreat. He left his mark as well on tactics, particularly on two of his favorite manoeuvres: either swift assaults on unexpected places in the enemy's line (the rear, the flanks, the lines of communication), which enveloped the foe (as in the battle of Ulm); or, sometimes at the risk of undermanning his own flanks, throwing massed infantry at the foe's center and overwhelming him (as at Austerlitz).

Napoleon innovated less in the tactical use of arms, merely remaining loyal to the lessons of the revolutionary wars. Combat was opened by the "wearing phase": free fire by sharpshooters spread out in front of the heavy battalions of the French line. Then came the decisive attack: Napoleon threw fresh forces either at the flanks, using a detached corps arriving from a distant point (as at Jena and Auerstaedt), or in overwhelming the enemy's wing (as at Austerlitz), or in pressing his center (as at Wagram). To rupture the enemy's lines, Napoleon would send in the mass of his reserves after careful and heavy artillery preparation. Then would come a systematic exploitation of the foe's retreat. Now cavalry played the principal role, often exterminating the enemy (as at Jena and Auerstaedt). After 1809, as the manoeuvering capabilities of his armies declined, Napoleon tended to cut short the "wearing phase" of battle, opting for direct assault by heavy, compact battalions even though enemy fire fearfully decimated French forces. Or, he would exploit the superior French fire power, concentrated on whatever objective was to be taken, thus enlarging the already great importance of artillery in French victories (as at Wagram and Borodino).

As it stood, the Napoleonic system of war had its limitations. Above all it suited wealthy countries, where the army could provision itself from the conquered land, where theaters of operation were not extensive (such as northern Italy or southern Germany) so that the foe could not escape, and where the emperor could more easily juggle all his corps. Terrible miscalculations took place on the immense and barren plains of eastern Europe. The system worked best when the emperor had only to confront armies of the Old Regime, when the enemy showed itself incapable of learning from its defeats and changing its methods, and mostly when the defeated peoples complied without budging.

2. Holding the Continent (1804–1809)

Despite English mastery of the seas, Napoleon's striking victories over the two coalitions permitted him to reorganize western Europe to his taste, thus striving to ruin Britain with a continental blockade. To maintain peace on the Continent and to better close it off to English goods, the emperor allied himself with the tsar. But the blockade dragged him into armed interventions, territorial annexations, and exploitations that finally exasperated the defeated peoples. Austria took avantage of the war in Spain to resurrect a coalition, though it was broken at Wagram. The continental system was thereafter at its height.

The Third Coalition and the Extension of the Continental System (1805–1806)

At first the war dragged. In part this was because there was no common theater of operations where the adversaries could meet, and in part it was because both England and France were in the midst of a financial crisis. To offset the 1804 deficit, Napoleon had to restore, under the innocent name of "unified duties," certain highly unpopular indirect (excise) taxes that the Revolution had abolished.

In order to invade England with the 150,000 men encamped at Boulogne, France had to control the English Channel. At the head of the Franco-Spanish fleet, Admiral Villeneuve was ordered to undertake this operation, but he let himself get blockaded in the harbor at Cadiz by an English squadron under the command of Lord Nelson. Earlier, in August 1804, the tsar had broken with Napoleon on the pretext of the continued presence of French troops beyond the Alps and the Rhine. Now, a year later, Alexander I signed an alliance with the British aimed at pushing France back to its 1792 borders. Austria, discontented over the Milan coronation, the annexation of the Ligurian Republic by France, and the creation of the Republic of Lucca for Napoleon's sister, Elisa, joined the Anglo-Russian alliance, and was soon followed by Sweden and the Kingdom of Naples. But the French emperor did not sit back and wait for his enemies to march. Suddenly, on 29 August 1805, he struck camp at Boulogne, and with incredible speed marched the *Grande Armée* of 150,000 to the Rhine. Meanwhile, he gave Admiral Villeneuve new orders to cover the Neapolitan coasts.

One reason to move rapidly was that in France the war was not popular. The opposition movement, though weaker than in the pre-Marengo era, was now very much alive. The putative rallied royalists sneered at Napoleon's grand designs, while the familiar hot spots of insurrection in the Midi and the west erupted again in flames. Fouché swiftly exposed several plots and summarily executed several royalist agents. At the same time France was shaken by a serious financial crisis. Momentarily straitened circumstances at the treasury were seriously magnified by the misdeeds of a group of munitions manufacturers and traffickers, led by the banker Ouvrard. Their speculations on the Spanish piaster provoked a public panic in financial circles, as people feared that the notes of the Bank of France would become as inflated and worthless as the revolutionary *assignats*. Only military victory restored confidence.

The *Grande Armée* (so named in October 1805) was an instrument of great quality. A quarter of its soldiers were veterans whose enlistment dated back as far as the Convention. Half the men had fought in the Italian campaign of 1800, and, for once, the new conscripts were fully trained. The troops were commanded by young marshals who, though they had received their batons only in 1804, had proven themselves under fire. The 1805 campaign was conducted with stunning speed and precision. French troops were joined by soldiers sent by several German states on the Rhine and the Main, as well as by Baden, Bavaria, and Wurtemberg. Taken utterly by surprise, the Austrian army under the command of General von Mack was surrounded by the French and capitulated without a struggle on 20 October. The very next day, however, Lord Nelson set aright the allied loss of face by virtually exterminating Villeneuve's Franco-Spanish fleet at Trafalgar. Napoleon now lost any chance of dictating a peace to London. But he did get the jump on the Russian army and entered Vienna before they could stop him. On 2 December, the anniversary of his coronation, the French emperor and his soldiers met the combined Russian and Austrian armies at a small village in Moravia, Austerlitz, where Napoleon brought off a stunning victory against more numerous forces than his own. The Russian army was virtually cut in two and driven into the Telnitz marshes. Austria withdrew from the coalition and sued for peace.

Napoleon, aware that Prussia had stood poised to join the coalition if the Austro-Russian armies had won, now persuaded the Prussians to ally themselves with the French. The two powers signed an accord on 16 December. Prussia received the right to annex Hanover (a British territory) in return for ceding Neuchâtel and Cleves to France. More important in Napoleon's eyes, Prussia was obliged to close her ports and markets to British goods.

Austria had no choice but to accept the humiliating treaty of Presburg, which eliminated her altogether from Germany and Italy. She abandoned the Tyrol and Vorarlberg to Bavaria, and turned over her Swabian possessions to Baden and Wurtemburg. She also ceded Venice to the Kingdom of Italy, and Dalmatia and Istria to France. (The later cessions were primarily intended to close off further coasts and ports to the British.) Meanwhile treaties of perpetual alliance were signed between France and, respectively, Baden, Bavaria, and Wurtemburg. (The last two duchies were promoted to kingdoms.) Bavaria ceded the Duchy of Berg to France. Marshal Murat, named duke of Cleves and Berg, became an elector of the Holy Roman Empire. As for the Kingdom of the Two Sicilies, Napoleon decreed from the Schoenbrunn Palace on 26 December,

"The dynasty of Naples has ceased to reign." Forthwith, Marshal Masséna occupied that country. Neapolitan—and, for that matter, pontifical—ports were immediately closed to English commerce.

For the next ten months—until October 1806—hostilities ceased in Europe, except for southern Italy, where Joseph Bonaparte, now king of Naples, faced armed insurrection from some of his subjects supported by the British. Later, British troops landed in Italy and routed the French general Reynier at Maida. For the first time the English commander used the devastating tactic of crossed artillery salvoes, an innovation the French would overlook to their detriment in Spain and at Waterloo. Soon all of Calabria was in arms, requiring all of Masséna's forces to be put down. Meanwhile the economic war between England and France continued. By February 1806, Prussia closed off the port of Lubeck and the Elbe, Weser, and Ems estuaries to British ships. French tariff laws renewed the prohibition on British products and taxed all other imports at an exhorbitant rate. London replied by extending and improving its naval blockade of continental ports from Brest to Lubeck.

During the intermission following Presburg, Napoleon profoundly reorganized the enormous portion of Europe under French influence. He acted in accord with the same political design he was applying in France: remolding society along the lines of the Old Regime. In effect, since his coronation, Napoleon no longer saw himself as "the revolution on the march," but rather as part of the family of kings. To legitimize his power in the eyes of monarchical Europe, he made matrimonial alliances with the reigning families. In January 1806, he married off Josephine's son, Eugène de Beauharnais (whom he had adopted) to the daughter of the king of Bavaria. Soon after, his cousin, Stephanie, was wed to the heir to the throne of Baden.

Napoleon believed that the continental system, aimed at English shipping, would be the better applied in the measure that he exercised influence over Europe's sovereigns. Thus, he handed out thrones to his brothers and sisters, save for Lucien, with whom he had broken. Holland went to Louis; Eugène was proclaimed viceroy of Italy; Joseph Bonaparte was constrained to accept the crown of Naples (together with the mission to retake Sicily). Elisa reigned as princess of Lucca and Piombino, while in March of the following year, Marshal Murat, now the husband of Caroline Bonaparte, became duke of Cleves and Berg. The decree of 30 March 1806, concerning the French imperial family, made a bow (and nothing more) to the Revolution's principle of equality, stipulating grandly, "The status of persons called to reign over this vast empire, and to strengthen it with marital alliances, is absolutely no different from that of any other Frenchmen." This was far from the last time that revolutionary tradition would be honored in the breach with empty words.

Indeed after 1806 in Italy, and 1807 in Germany, treaties concluded by the emperor put at his disposition a portion of the lands held personally by the reigning families of various states. These lands and their incomes were distributed as endowments to members of Napoleon's family, to dignitaries of the empire, and to soldiers whom the emperor wished to reward. These awards, coupled with the other measures, succeeded in creating in France a new social hierarchy. In March 1806, nineteen "grand fiefs of the empire" were established variously in the kingdoms of Italy and Naples, in the principalities of Piombino, and in the states of Parma and Plaisance. Such fiefs, though conferring no political rights on their holders, consisted of a noble title, revenues from the land, and stipends from the state treasury of the country in which the fief was located. Two papal possessions were confiscated in the Kingdom of Naples, promoted to the principalities of Ponte-Corvo and Benevento, and given to Marshal Bernadotte and to Talleyrand.

To finance his social designs, Napoleon further imposed on his Italian satellites measures aimed at skimming monies from their national treasuries and financial establishments. Thus, for example, the Mont-de-Piété bank in Milan had to pay annual fees of 1,200,000 francs to a list of soldiers of all grades chosen by Napoleon. These states also had to furnish troops, warships, and even workers, and generally had to comply strictly to the French imperial project. This meant of course the rigorous prohibition against importing English goods, or for that matter any goods manufactured abroad, while simultaneously according a special, preferred status to French goods. Napoleon sought to force the pope to adhere to these policies in the church states, but he energetically refused. Thus commenced an endless, draining conflict between emperor and pontiff.

Napoleon also made major changes in the constitution of Germany. On 16 July 1806, France joined with sixteen states—including the two kingdoms (Bavaria and Wurtemburg) and the three grand duchies (Baden, Hesse-Darmstadt, and Berg and Cleves)—to sign a treaty that founded the Confederation of the Rhine. The German signatories separated themselves in perpetuity from the old Holy Roman Empire, forming instead a "particular confederation" under the protection of the French emperor. Another treaty between France and the sixteen states, "taken collectively and separately," created an alliance among the contracting parties such that, if any one of them would be at war, the confederation would immediately field 63,000 soldiers, to be placed under the command of its imperial French protector. The latter, in his turn, was obliged to field 200,000 in the service of "German independence." France could also permanently station troops in Germany. Under the circumstances, the Austrian emperor was forced to abolish the centuries-old Holy Roman Empire of the German nation. Outside more enlightened circles, many voices were raised to protest these transformations. Indeed anti-Napoleonic pamphlets circulated in abundance. As an example to other booksellers who dealt in such literature, the French government ordered one of their number in Nuremberg, a certain Palm, to be tried. He was found guilty and shot. Although most German intellectuals had shown themselves favorable to Napoleon when he was First Consul, they now saw in him nothing but a despot. Their opinion, however, was far from unanimous.

In the short time of ten months, Napoleon had succeeded in building on the French homeland a Grand Empire, a federation of states organized along French lines and subordinated to French designs. But already discontent against French domination was starting to manifest itself, notably in Naples and in Germany.

The Fourth Coalition and the Beginning of the Continental Blockade (1806–1807)

Prussia, too, was annoyed by the formation of the Confederation of the Rhine. The war party in Berlin, led by Queen Louise, ended by getting the upper hand on the pro-French forces at the Prussian court. On 1 October 1806, therefore,

Napoleon received from King Frederick William III an ultimatum: either the French retire from Germany or war would ensue. Less than two weeks later, the Prussian army no longer existed. As usual for the French, the campaign was an improvised affair, yet military operations were so vigorously pursued that the war was over before the *Grande Armée* could suffer from its lack of preparations. On 14 October, Prussia was twice crushed: at Jena, by Napoleon himself, and at Auerstedt, by Marshal Davout. The debris of the army was pitilessly pursued through the length of north Germany. Prussia's fortresses collapsed one by one. The emperor entered Berlin while his army occupied the whole of Prussia except for its easternmost provinces.

Napoleon now decided to make himself the master of the entire German littoral to better combat English commerce. Despite their neutrality, the Hanseatic port cities were thus occupied by French troops. Everywhere British goods and ships were seized. Master—in theory, anyway—of the most crucial centers of English continental commerce, the Baltic and North Sea coasts, Napoleon thus imagined he had delivered the decisive stroke. Europe after all had customarily absorbed nearly a third of English exports and about a third of her industrial production. Closing the Continent could thus deliver a severe, if perhaps not fatal, blow to British industry. It would at the same time deprive English consumers of the Continent's grains and the Royal Navy of the Baltics' munitions. Finally, Napoleon gambled on the fragility of British balance of payments, the threat of the uncontrollable inflation of Britain's paper currency. Although the actual conditions for the success of his plan were far from being created, Napoleon thought the time was right. On 21 November 1806, from Berlin, he proclaimed his famous decree: "The British Isles are declared subject to a state of blockade." This was the birth certificate of the so-called continental blockade, which may be defined as the collective name given to all of the measures—political, military, diplomatic—taken unilaterally by Napoleon and forced upon the states of Europe, aimed at squeezing British commerce. The European governments were not consulted about this decree but had no choice except to adhere to its provisions. Its immediate application in Holland, Spain, Napoleonic Italy, and the Hanseatic towns thus not surprisingly saw the simultaneous appearance of a prodigious market in contraband via Hamburg, Tonningen, Gibraltar, and Malta. Only the return of peace permitted imperial authorities to mount a coastal surveillance sufficient to close off most of this black market.

Particularly since the reappearance of *chouannerie* uprisings in the west and Normandy, French public opinion desired peace. The Russians, despite Austerlitz, were not willing to open treaty negotiations, so Napoleon marched into Poland. Immediately it became clear that his method of war was poorly adapted to eastern Europe, with its severe climate and its immense plains, where enemy armies could more easily strike and get away, and where the land was too poor for effective marauding. Moreover, the French emperor found himself confronted with yet another problem: the Polish question. Local patriots expected nothing less from him than the resurrection of an independent nation. Napoleon, needing troops, let the Poles raise him legions, thus encouraging them to hope for a reward, but he promised nothing. The truth was that as long as he desired a lasting peace with Russia, Prussia, and Austria, Napoleon could not for a second envisage reconstituting Poland. His time in Poland was not wasted, however, for he met there the beautiful countess Marie Waleswka and, by producing a child with her, made the discovery that Josephine, not he, was responsible for the childlessness of their marriage. The avenue to a divorce was now open.

Meanwhile the winter campaign was arduous. The battle of Eylau (8 February 1807) amounted to butchery: 25,000 Russians and 18,000 French casualties. Napoleon could not pursue the defeated foe. The following day, for the first time, angry murmurs were heard in the French ranks when the emperor passed, while on the home front public opinion was stupefied by such huge losses in such a short time. Another first: the year 1807 saw the first anticipatory conscription. Fully 80,000 men from the "class" of 1808 were inducted, and foreign allies were demanded to reinforce their contingents. Meanwhile, the now considerably elongated lines of military communications created their own difficulties. Still, the formidable French artillery allowed Napoleon to score a decisive victory over the Russians at Friedland (14 June 1807). The French, already masters of Danzig, now entered Königsberg.

Both belligerents ardently wished for peace. Highly displeased with what he saw as the passivity of Austria and England, Tsar Alexander I hoped to divide Europe between himself and Napoleon. The French emperor, for his part, was not eager to engage his troops further on the eastern steppes. He was already concerned about his vulnerable communication lines, which extended deep into Austrian dominions. Mostly, though, he was obsessively intent upon sealing off the Continent the more tightly to English commerce. Out of the meeting of the emperor and the tsar came the accords signed at Tilsit (7 July 1807): a peace treaty containing secret clauses, and a military alliance to which, two days later, Prussia adhered.

The treaty was pitiless toward Prussia. She lost all her provinces west of the Elbe. These joined the Confederation of the Rhine as the Kingdom of Westphalia, under the scepter of Jerome Bonaparte. An even larger segment of Prussian provinces, formerly part of Poland, was now reformed as the Grand Duchy of Warsaw. This sop to the Poles meant relatively little, however, for the protector of the duchy was a German, the sovereign of Saxony, now raised to the dignity of king. Creating the Grand Duchy did little, of course, to reassure Alexander I. The first of many shadows was cast over the new Franco-Russian alliance. What remained of Prussia bent under occupation by the *Grande Armée* until the government of Frederick William paid a crushing war indemnity. Russia turned over to France Cattaro and the Ionian islands, adhered to the continental blockade, and generally promised to act toward England in accordance with Napoleon's designs. In exchange, Alexander received a free hand in the Turkish empire and in Finland, which was then part of the Kingdom of Sweden. French power in Europe thus attained its apogee, yet the coming of peace did not assuage all concerns in France—not least because the *Grande Armée*, between the camp of Boulogne and the battlefield of Friedland, had suffered 35,000 killed and 150,000 wounded (half so badly that they would never march again).

The Blockade, Iberian Problems, and the Fifth Coalition (1809)

The tsar, as expected, offered his mediation to try to bring about peace between England and France. The British replied by bombarding Copenhagen and capturing the Danish fleet (September 1807). Russia then declared war on England, while Denmark and Austria formally adhered to the blockade. With the tsar playing his favorite role of policeman of southern Europe, Napoleon could concentrate his vigilance on the Mediterranean. Prince Eugène was ordered to occupy the littoral of the Papal States and to firmly apply the Berlin Decree. Meanwhile the Queen of Etruria, who had allowed Livorno to become a black market of English merchandise, was dispossessed of her state, which Napoleon promptly turned over to his sister. Elisa became a grand duchess, her dominion part of the French Empire.

Portugal, which had always refused to adhere to the blockade, permitted its ports to serve as centers of British contraband. Napoleon made an accord with the Spanish king and his chief minister, Godolphin, for the partition of their small neighbor. Marshal Junot marched his army across Spain and occupied Portugal with no difficulty, taking Lisbon on 30 November 1807. The reigning family, the Baraganzas, fled to Brazil, thus opening a new South American port to the British. One long-term effect of the Portuguese matter was to promote Latin American independence.

The British orders in council of November 1807 required all neutral merchant vessels destined for European ports to pass by a British-controlled port for inspection. Here they must pay a tax, obtain a license, and take aboard British contraband. Napoleon replied to the audacity of the "oceanocrats" with the Milan Decree (November–December 1807). After this, all neutral shipping that had passed by any British port would not be permitted to disembark on the Continent.

Because Sweden refused to participate in the blockade, early in 1808 the tsar seized Finland. But this did not really prevent the British from controlling the Baltic Sea. Pope Pius VII showed something less than zeal in adhering to Napoleon's continental system, so General Miollis was ordered to occupy Rome, which he did on 2 February 1808. The pope also lost Ancona to the newly fashioned Kingdom of Italy. Now the European continent was more sealed off to Britain than it had ever been, or would ever be again. Even contraband was no longer obtainable in quantity. On the other side of the channel, industrial production declined, bringing unemployment and upheaval in its wake. Still, it did not bring the social revolution that Napoleon had hoped for. The situation might have indeed become critical for the British if the closure had continued for any length of time, but it did not. England was saved.

With the occupation of Portugal, Napoleon had finally set foot in Iberia. For some time he had been of the opinion—not entirely baseless—that Spain was poorly governed. He had also convinced himself that the Spanish would submit to French regeneration of their country. Under the pretext of securing his ties with his army in Portugal, he increased French military presence in Spain. On 18 March 1808, a riot broke out in Madrid and King Charles IV was forced to abdicate. The people called his son Ferdinand to the throne. Less than a week later, Marshal Murat entered Madrid. Observing that the Spanish throne was now legally vacant, Napoleon moved to place a Bonaparte upon it. Claiming that anarchy was ravaging the country, he summoned the old king and his son to a meeting at Bayonne. But on 2 May the people of Madrid rioted to prevent their crown prince from attending. Murat, supported by a terrified Spanish bourgeoisie, drowned the insurrection in blood, and the Bayonne meeting went forward. The French obtained a double abdication from the Spanish Bourbons. The decree of 10 July 1808 named Joseph Bonaparte king of Spain. (He was replaced in Naples by Murat.) A commission of Spanish notables, belonging to the "enlightened" (pro-French) milieux, was convened to draw up a constitution.

At the news of the Bayonne meeting, the Spanish people, with the active support of the Catholic clergy and the nobility, rose in generalized revolt against the French "heretics" and "persecutors of the pope," and against the political and social regime that they intended to found. In short, Spain became a new Vendée—heroic and retrograde. Everywhere juntas sprang up to give leadership to the rebellion. In Seville, a local junta even declared formal war on the French. For the first time Napoleon found himself on the wrong side of a war of national liberation, a war that defied all the known rules and strategies. On 22 July, General Dupont surrendered at Baylen. The insurrection grew. A month later, Joseph was forced to quit the capital, which was in open rebellion. The uprisings soon reached Portugal, where English troops arrived under Wellesley, the future duke of Wellington. At the end of August, they met Junot at Cintra and defeated him decisively. Baylen and Cintra were the first real defeats the French had met with during the empire. They coincided, moreover, with the discovery in Paris of a republican plot against Napoleon, led by General Malet and supported by La Fayette as well as many liberal senators.

Convinced that the defeats were the fault of his lieutenants, Napoleon decided to lead the *Grande Armée* in person to Spain and restore the status quo. To do so, he had to take great care to protect his rear, for Austria, with English gold, was already quietly re-arming itself. He thus needed the assistance that Tsar Alexander had promised at Tilsit.

The Franco-Russian sovereigns met at Erfurt from 27 September to 14 October 1808, in the presence of all the princes of the Confederation of the Rhine. Napoleon erred in bringing Talleyrand with him to the meeting, for he was secretly counseling the tsar to "save Europe by standing up to Napoleon." He had also alerted Austria to his master's intentions. The French emperor obtained from his Russian counterpart only the vague promise of eventual assistance against Austria, in return for which Napoleon had to make real concessions: to evacuate part of Prussia, reduce its war indemnity, and to allow the tsar to retain Finland and the Danubian provinces. But at least the emperor believed he had before him the few months necessary to conclude the Spanish affair.

On 12 October 1808, the *Grande Armée*, as such, went out of existence. A contingent of 100,000 of its men remained in Germany as the Army of the Rhine. With the remaining 180,000, augmented by 30,000 men of the guard, Napoleon himself entered Spain. The troops he took with him were on the whole hardened veterans, including some strong and experienced German and Polish contingents. Napoleon seized the pass at Somosierra on 30 November and opened the route to Madrid. When he arrived in the capital, he re-installed Joseph, abolished feudal rights and the Inquisition, and suppressed two-thirds of Spain's convents. But his enemy was not vanquished. Spain was not conquered.

In January of 1809, the emperor was forced to leave
Spain after learning that Austria had re-armed and Paris
was alive with conspiracies. Fouché and Talleyrand had
formed a traitorous alliance aimed at replacing Napoleon
with Murat. The stock exchange fell sharply. Napoleon re-
established some order in Paris by relieving Talleyrand of
his duties, but when he left for Germany, he left behind a
France mined by doubt and treachery.

In the spring of 1809, Austria, having modernized her
army and knowing (through Talleyrand's activities) that the
tsar would not budge, prepared to attack Napoleon. She
carried with her this time the hopes of the German patriots,
those romantics whose national conscience had been sharp-
ened by the French occupation. Before marching on Bavaria,
the Austrian commander, Archduke Charles, issued an
"Appeal to the German Nation," written by Frederic
Schlege, that declared, "We shall fight to give Germany her
independence and her national honor."

Napoleon was obliged to improvise a new army
quickly. Its ranks were one-third foreigners (especially German loyalists and Italians), and most of the troops were
poorly trained conscripts. The campaign soon demonstrated
their inaptitude for manoeuvre. Their unreliability in combat reflected their lack of instruction. To compensate for the
low quality of his men, Napoleon augmented his materiel,
bringing with him 6,000 cannon from Spain.

Austria was counting on a general uprising in Germany, but such proved to be a premature hope, for many
German princes stood by their alliances with Napoleon.
Popular murmuring was nonetheless heard in more than
one state of the Confederation of the Rhine. Even before
the opening of official hostilities, Katte, an ex-officer of the

Prussian royal army, tried to stage a popular putsch with 300 men in the Kingdom of Westphalia. He met with defeat, but on 10 April 1809, a small hotel owner in the Tyrol, Andreas Hofer, staged a Vendée-style uprising among the local peasants against the Bavarian masters and their French allies.

The military campaign of 1809 was brutal. Marshal Davout threw the Austrians out of Bavaria with a brilliant turning manoeuvre that led to a victory at Eckmühl (22 April). The Archduke Charles just managed to save his army from complete destruction. The same day, a colonel in King Jerome Bonaparte's personal guard led an uprising in Westphalia, but it, too, failed.

On 12 May, Napoleon again entered Vienna, where he was greeted with bad news: Marshal Poniatowski had retreated in Poland, and Prince Eugène was defeated in Italy. Murat, meanwhile, sent word that the English had disembarked in Naples, and Rome was alive with agitation. Angered, Napoleon immediately annexed the Papal States to France. It was the end of even the appearance of an alliance with the church.

Napoleon now sought to use against Austria the same arm used against him in Spain and Germany: the national uprising. But the emperor's appeal to the Hungarians to constitute themselves as a separate nation (separate from Austria) met with no echo. Instead, Napoleon had to take to the field to vanquish the Archduke Charles. But first he had to cross the Danube, whose bridges had been destroyed. Hoping to cross from the north bank, he was pushed back by Charles at Aspern and at Essling. At the latter battle Marshal Lannes was killed; moreover, the personal military prestige of the emperor was now challenged.

Peasant uprisings immediately ensued in Wurtemberg and Hesse-Darmstadt. The "black legion" of the Prince of Brunswick-Oels, equipped by Austria, occupied Dresden, Leipzig, and Bayreuth. Indeed it presently crossed the breadth of Germany to the North Sea, where it was spirited away by British ships to fight again against the French in Spain. Meanwhile, in Italy Marshal MacDonald restored French authority, thereby allowing Prince Eugène to take the field from the south against the Austrians. On 10 June, Pius VII excommunicated Napoleon, who in turn made him a prisoner at Savona. The French clergy, however, apparently remained calm. The next month, a dearly bought victory over the Austrians at Wagram righted the general situation for Napoleon. On 12 July, Austria signed an armistice at Znaim that permitted Marshal Lefebvre and General Drouet-d'Erlon to reconquer the Tyrol.

The English, under Wellesley, were anything but inactive. They chased Marshal Soult from Portugal, and on 30 July 1809, they landed in the Low Countries, taking Flessigen and threatening Antwerp. In Paris, Fouché, interim Minister of the Interior, acting on his own authority, raised 30,000 national guards. French public opinion suddenly awakened. It seemed like 1793, the more so as the man in power (Fouché) was a regicide of the convention. He handed power over this citizen army to Marshal Bernadotte, who had been in disgrace for his passivity at Wagram. The call for the national guard, meanwhile, had provoked a counteraction in the Sarre. Order was soon enough re-established, but only at the price of many executions. Once the English evacuated the Low Countries, Napoleon gave the order to disband the national guard, for he deeply suspected the Fouché-Bernadotte alliance. In Paris, it seemed to him, plenty of people were always thinking about candidates to succeed him, whether Murat, Eugène, or Joseph. Somehow from his prison cell, General Malet had managed to hatch a new republican plot, which the police discovered; while in Provence, the royalists, along with ex-convention member Barras, contacted the British fleet. Much to the royalists' delight, Catholics, especially in the Belgian departments of the empire, expressed discontent over the pope's imprisonment. And on 13 October, at the Schoenbrunn Palace outside Vienna, a Saxon tried to assassinate Napoleon.

The peace of Vienna, signed on 6 October 1809, was humiliating for Austria. She ceded Galicia to the Grand Duchy of Warsaw, Salzburg to Bavaria, and all her Adriatic provinces to Napoleon, who now got his hands on one of the main routes of the oriental cotton trade. By the end of 1809 the military situation was completely redressed—even in Spain, where Wellington had had to fall back on Portugal (though this did not prevent Napoleon from reinforcing Massena with 100,000 more men, including his Young Guard).

For the blockade, however, the situation was far less brilliant. From the middle of 1808 on, the demands of his Iberian problems had obliged Napoleon to cut back the forces stationed along the North Sea and the Baltic. The reductions increased in 1809, when men had had to be assembled en masse along the Danube. Worse, Portugal, Spain, Brazil, Latin America, and, soon, the United States reopened their ports to British trade—so much that Great Britain's industrial production for that year attained a level unknown before the blockade!

Napoleon was well aware of this blow to his plans, as he was of the havoc created for the French economy by his continental system. For the French cotton industry to obtain the vital raw materials it needed, and to permit large French agricultural producers to export wheat, wine, and liqueurs, the emperor set up a licensing system for French shipowners. They could now send flour, grains, wines, and liqueurs to England on condition that their vessels return with an equivalent value in colonial raw materials, cotton, and wool. This measure, however, not only profited England more than France, it infuriated Napoleon's continental allies, for its articles applied exclusively to French merchants.

The year 1809 ended with a coup de théâtre: on 16 December, a Senate decree announced the dissolution of the marriage contract between Napoleon and Josephine.

CHAPTER 4

Napoleon I and the Revolution

ith his coronation oath, Napoleon assumed the obligation to defend the territorial conquests of the Revolution. On this score, he had more than kept his word. The France of the so-called natural frontiers had comprised 102 departments, and the Napoleonic empire in 1812 comprised 130 departments over 750,000 square kilometers, stretching from the Baltic Sea to the Turkish empire and peopled by 40 million souls. On the other hand, concerning revolutionary principles, Napoleon remained in the eyes of Europe "the Revolution on the march," but in France he betrayed much of the political and social heritage of the Revolution.

1. The Revolution Betrayed by the Empire

The emperor never ceased accentuating the autocratic character of his government. Physically Napoleon had changed. Already on his return from Tilsit his hairline was noticeably receding while his face was filling out, along with his belly. True, in the midst of the opulence of his court, he preserved a personal taste for the simple life, and until 1810–1811, he remained an extraordinary workaholic. Age perhaps, or the disillusions inflicted on him by his family and close collaborators, made him increasingly less willing to lean on others or to take counsel from his most competent advisors. Egoism made a more exaggerated appearance in his personality now, as did a taste for violence, contempt for people, and a blind ambition and self-confidence. These qualities drove him toward increasingly imprudent enterprises. Finally, he began to lose the instinct he had once had for sensing the deepest hopes and feelings of public opinion.

The divorce from Josephine was dictated by dynastic concerns: the need for an heir and to put an end to the intrigues of his family and entourage concerning the succession. It was no less dictated by Napoleon's strong wish to ensure a lasting peace by marrying into a family of established reigning monarchs. Actually, the marriage to the Austrian archduchess was a fallback measure taken when the tsar refused Napoleon the hand of a Russian princess. As Metternich was looking for an opportunity to break up the strong Franco-Russian alliance, it was a simple matter for Napoleon to be betrothed to the eighteen-year-old Marie Louise. On what turned out, ironically, to be the anniversary of the execution of the duc d'Enghien (2 April 1810), the French emperor married the grand niece of Marie-Antoinette and Louis XVI. In France, the heirs of 1789 and 1793 did not try to hide their hostility, and many of Napoleon's soldiers reproached him for divorcing his "old lady" [*sa vieille*]. Still forming marital links to the ancient House of Habsburg and the birth of an heir (the king of Rome, on 20 March 1811) seemed to have guaranteed the future of this, the fourth, dynasty to reign in France, as well as the peace of Europe.

The emperor had already begun to purge his entourage of all the strong personalities who had come out of the Revolution (for example, he replaced Talleyrand with the docile Champagny). Now, with his new marriage, the last holdouts of the Revolution disappeared from the higher spheres of government, many to be replaced by former aristocrats of the Old Regime who had rallied to the empire. In June of 1810, the dismissal of Fouché represented the final break with the personnel inherited from the Revolution. Administrative power ultimately absorbed every other kind of power, including that of the elected assemblies. Even at the level of the canton, the elective bodies where universal suffrage had been the practice were no longer convoked. In the formation of the electoral colleges at departmental levels, the nomination of candidates by central administrative authority came to take precedence over election, to the benefit of the nobility, large property holders, and high-level bureaucrats. In sum, the legislative branch of government became nothing but a decoration. With the suppression of the Tribunate in 1807, all discussion of issues ceased. The sessions of the Legislative Body became briefer. The emperor himself legislated more and more by personal and senatorial decree, particularly in matters of military conscription. The Senate saw its aristocratic character accentuated. The high salaries, large land grants, and the hope of even further imperial gifts rendered the senators completely docile.

Political and administrative centralization became all the more rigorous, and, even if a former member of the Committee of Public Safety such as Jean-Bon Saint-André remained in his prefect's post at Mainz until 1813, the prefectoral corps was becoming infiltrated by members of the old aristocracy. Increasing, too, was the number of prefects who had come to their jobs from the Council of State. In the last analysis, administrative centralization during the empire encountered no other obstacles than the slowness of communication and the inertia of those administered.

Justice lost its independence and was reorganized to augment the aristocratic tendencies of the regime. Despite the assumption that judges could not be removed, successive purges of the judicial corps from 1808 to 1810 domesticated this institution. Many of the new magistrates came from the parlements of the Old Regime. Special courts increasingly took over cases from regular courts. In 1810, for example, thirty-four tribunals and eight provost courts were created to consider contraband cases. The judgments handed down—including branding and death sentences—were unappealable. The codification of the laws, undertaken by the consulate, went forward, only now in a spirit increasingly opposed to the principles of the Revolution. Thus, the Penal Code of 1810 revived barbaric punishments such as the iron collar and branding, and the Code of Criminal Procedure suppressed grand juries and replaced them with secret examination procedures.

The omnipotence of the police under Savary (who replaced Fouché) held individual liberties in check. The police carefully oversaw all expression of opinion; the "black cabinet" audited private correspondence. The gendarmerie and the agents of ministers, prefects, and the emperor himself competed with one another in their zeal for informing and internal espionage. Police repression, moreover, was beyond the reach of the judiciary. All opposition to the emperor was intently scrutinized; people were held arbitrarily without warrants in state prisons or in mental asylums. Freedom of opinion disappeared. Official censorship tolerated no criticism, not even veiled, of the emperor or his policies. Madame de Staël and Chateaubriand figured among the more illustrious victims. The decrees of 1810 left alive but one newspaper per department and four in Paris— all were required to be guided in their views by the official *Le Moniteur* and all were surveyed by a corps of inspectors whose salaries were paid by the papers themselves. In sum, French newspapers of the era amounted to a press of "beck and call." As for printers and booksellers, they had to request a revocable license and take an oath to get it.

So there remained nothing of the fundamental freedoms that the Revolution had defined, except perhaps religious and economic liberty. Yet the French were all the more resigned to autocratic government, as the Old Regime and the Revolution had accustomed them to it. On the other hand, it must be said that although it was authoritarian, the empire was not bloody. What, after all, were 2,500 people held arbitrarily in prison (as of 1814) compared to the multitudes of suspects imprisoned and beheaded during the Terror?

Despotism was no less noticeable in governance that employed intellectuals and artists. Napoleon always displayed true genius in the art of propaganda. He had a remarkable ability to use every means of communication— newspapers, army bulletins, church sermons, and popular imagery. Such great artists as David, Géricault, Gros, and Proudhon were mobilized for service to the regime. Like the Roman emperors before him, Napoleon developed his own style of triumphal architecture, whose principal elements were the arch and the column. To firmly anchor his myth with the common people, he invented an entire imperial cult, with its own liturgical calendar of regular and improvised feast days (Napoleon's birthday, the anniversary of the coronation, the baptism of the king of Rome, etc). The visit of the imperial couple to this or that region boasted its own ritual: a religious service, an official banquet convoking all the local notables, outdoor games, alms distributed to the poor, fireworks, and sometimes even the marriage of a local queen of the May, who received a dowry from the emperor, to a worthy veteran of the *Grande Armée*.

Education remained more than ever an instrument of rule for Napoleon. It was oriented toward "respect for religion and love of the sovereign" and "the glorious history of our fourth dynasty." The imperial university, established in 1808, held a legal monopoly over all levels of instruction. Private institutions were not tolerated except by special authorization, and even then they were overseen by the university and had to pay a special tax to it. Although ecclesiastics held positions at all levels of the university's hierarchy, the institution's methods and the propagandistic content of its teaching were well received by a large fraction of the more prosperous Frenchmen, many of whom were anticlerical. Still, not all worked according to plan. A significant number of wealthier families enrolled their children in private establishments. Where education was concerned, in short, the emperor largely failed to "control minds and hearts."

Neither did Napoleon fail to enroll the church in the service of his despotism. To that end, he poured out his attentions on her. Seminarians and priests were exempt from conscription, and religious instruction, although placed under episcopal authority, was made mandatory in elementary and high schools. But in exchange the clergy was expected to do the bidding of government; for example, to take a strong stand against deserters and draft dodgers. For children of more modest families, who did not attend elementary or high schools, the "imperial catechism" was set up in 1806 to teach children their duties to their emperor. In all ways, the Catholic clergy was associated with the imperial cult. Therefore, it was hardly surprising that the success of this politics of altar-in-service-of-throne was seriously compromised after 1809 by Napoleon's falling out with the pope.

As for the Revolution's social conquests, Napoleon broke with the principle that the French held dearest: equality. In the annexed department on the left bank of the Rhine and in Piedmont, a very high proportion (50 percent to 70 percent) of nationalized lands were withheld from public sale to endow senators and other imperial dignitaries. In the Hanseatic departments, annexed in 1810, certain feudal rights were abolished only at the price of monetary compensation. Finally, in the departments formed out of the Papal States, the Civil Code underwent important retouchings and finally was not really enforced at all.

Throughout the empire, Napoleon pursued his policy of re-establishing social hierarchies. His final "granite mass," as he termed these hierarchies, was the foundation of an imperial nobility. A nobility of individual (not family) title, the new institution was intended to blend the revolutionary bourgeoisie to the old aristocracy, whom Napoleon hoped to pry from its loyalty to the Bourbons. The new nobility was hereditary, yet different from the old in including notables and men of merit—the very men whom the emperor hoped to make forget about their loss of individual freedoms. At the lowest level, the Legion of Honor, though only a simple decoration, could be considered a sort of life-aristocracy. But the real titled nobility was created on 30 March, 1806, the date when the titles of prince and duke were accorded to members of the imperial family and to selected dignitaries of the empire. Thirty grand fiefs were established in Italy to endow the new nobles, among whom were Napoleon's marshals, many decorated with titles in honor of the battlefields where they had proved themselves. A third decisive step was taken when the Senate voted on 1 March 1808 to institute a nobility of civil service as well as a personal nobility. As the grand dignitaries and ministers with fiefs were dukes, the bureaucrats on the next rung, which included archbishops, became counts, and bishops and the mayors of France's thirty-seven largest cities assumed the title of baron. As for the patents of personal nobility, they were accorded by the emperor on a case-by-case basis to specific prefects, generals, and other deserving subjects.

The new nobility was considerably less numerous than the old, however. Of its 1,509 members, fifty-nine percent were drawn from the military, 22 percent were civil servants, and 17 percent were elected officials (such as senators and mayors). Unlike the old, it conferred no social privilege, no dispensations from any laws or taxes. Feudalism, in other words, was not re-established; indeed, the new titles were not hereditary, except in very special (and rare) cases. Thus did social inequality, in direct violation of the Civil Code, make its reappearance in France.

The new institution was a grave error, for it shocked public opinion. Moreover, in the measure that the new ti-tleholders turned out to be more a coterie of flattering courtiers than steadfast dynastic mainstays in times of crisis, the new institution worked to the disadvantage of their emperor.

2. The Revolution, Unfinished in Europe

It is as incorrect to imagine that Napoleon sought to spread the benefits of the Revolution from Guadalquivir to the Moskva as it is to imagine he could have done so if he had wanted to. His power to intervene in the internal affairs of states under French influence was not limitless, except in those governments run by his own family, or in the Grand Duchy of Warsaw. In other governments, he could impose his will only in foreign affairs, and, even then, he usually had to lead by example. To be sure, in the Duchy of Berg and the Kingdom of Westphalia, he constructed model states designed to convince the other princes of the superiority of the French system so forcefully that they would adopt it. Yet in no state, other than Warsaw and the states run by members of his family, did he impose the Civil Code. Where it was imposed, the transformation of state and society amounted to a more or less extensive revolution from on high with the civil administration being the architect. But if princes adopted this politics, it is safe to say that they did so with the aim of increasing their power or meeting French military and economic demands more easily.

Napoleon believed that state reform had to stand on a constitution. The Cisalpine and Luccan republics and Holland were endowed with such documents under the consulate and required only slight alteration when the empire was declared. Napoleon also promulgated constitutions in the other family-run states: Westphalia, Naples, Berg, and

Spain, as well as in the Grand Duchy of Warsaw. Bavaria, Baden, Frankfurt, and Anhalt-Coethen gave themselves constitutions along the French line, but except in Anhalt-Coethen and in the Kingdom of Italy, there was never a slavish imitation of the French model—though they did not fall too far from the mark.

Which is to say, executive power was reinforced everywhere. Where representative organs were created and the principle of national sovereignty was formally recognized, legislative initiative still remained in executive hands. Where national representation was instituted, the right to vote was nonetheless reserved for the more important citizens, though admittedly not according to any hereditary social hierarchy. The pretentions of the old feudal nobility to govern were swept away for all time. To be sure, a certain number of fundamental rights defined by the French Revolution were constitutionally introduced in lands that had never known them—rights that included the laicization of the state and of society, equality before the law, and the abolition of noble fiscal and judicial privilege, and of religious discrimination. By virtue of these principles, certain states took measures to emancipate their Jews.

For the most part, however, the states under the emperor's direct influence gave themselves technical, centralized, bureaucratized, and, above all, hierarchicalized administrations aimed at one thing: efficacy. In these states, taxes were paid more efficiently and justice was reformed, usually by separating it from politics. The nobility lost its former judicial prerogatives. Army recruitment was based more or less on universal conscription.

In the Josephist and revolutionary traditions, the majority of the new states placed the church squarely under the government's control, without even bothering to legislate a concordat with Rome. The clergy ceased to be a privileged order; its property was placed at the disposition of either the prince or the state, who in turn put most of it up for public sale. The number of convents was considerably reduced.

Certain states, however, remained obstinately true to the political, social, and administrative structures of the Old Regime. Nothing better demonstrates the limits of Napoleon's authority than the fact that an ally as loyal to France as was the Kingdom of Saxony stood in this group. In all states, social reform was less far-reaching than administrative. Diplomatic and military necessities required that Napoleon placate the princes and their aristocracies, which necessarily meant that he could not export the principles of 1789 *en bloc*. For example, he had to accept that the constitution of the Confederation of the Rhine expressly guaranteed the seigneurial and feudal rights of the annexed princes, a stipulation that set sharp limits to the abolition of feudalism elsewhere, even in member states governed by a French prince.

The Civil Code was enforced only in the kingdoms of Italy and Westphalia, the Illyrian provinces, and the three grand duchies of Berg, Frankfurt, and Warsaw. With considerable revising, it was exported to the Kingdom of Naples and the Grand Duchy of Baden. Often the local nobility succeeded in amending the constitution to protect their property and privileges. And where expropriation of seigneurial or feudal rights did occur, it was very often only "against a just and prior indemnity." In sum, the code all too frequently served only to preserve the social structures that it claimed to destroy.

In the same way, the social policies of the emperor in France sometimes contributed to halting the abolition of feudalism elsewhere. In the Italian states under Bonaparte rulers, as in Westphalia, Berg, and Warsaw, the revenues from the lands of the former royal domains were handed over to the owners of the grand fiefs and endowments were set up for French dignitaries. These endowments alone numbered 3,596, representing an annual revenue of about 30 million francs (780 million in today's francs [$135 million]). Such revenues came from fees and taxes that were unquestionably feudal or seigneurial in origin, for example, the *cens* and the *dîme*. To protect the value of the endowments, these fees and taxes were maintained. And because the principle of equality dictated that what was done on certain estates had to be done on all, many feudal or seigneurial rights were retained everywhere.

Whenever legislation actually suppressed land rents, it could happen only with compensation. The difficulty of determining the amount of compensation, and the diversity of solutions it required in some states delayed the abolition of feudalism. In general, seven solutions were adopted: (1) outright, total abolition, without compensation of personal servitude and feudal rights (as in the Kingdom of Italy); (2) total abolition of personal servitude and certain feudal rights, with compensation for certain others (as in Naples, the Swiss Confederation, and some Hanseatic departments); (3) total abolition of personal servitude with compensation for all feudal rights (as in Berg and Bavaria); (4) abolition of serfdom, compensation for the *corvée* and other feudal rights; (5) compensation for personal servitude (for serfdom in Hesse-Darmstedt and for the *corvée* in the Illyrian provinces); (6) abolition of serfdom, compensation for the *corvée*, the *dîme*, and certain feudal rights (as in Warsaw); and (7) abolition of serfdom with maintenance of land rents and the *corvée* (as in Baden and Wurtemberg). The *dîme* was maintained in Frankfurt. In sum, only serfdom was more or less completely abolished without compensation.

A significant improvement in the peasants' conditions would have entailed a profound alteration in land ownership. An effort was made to bring this about through the sale of ecclesiastical (and some royal) lands, but although we do not have enough specific regional studies to say with certainty who benefited from these sales, it would appear that by and large the buyers of the lands were those who already owned them.

In other words, the peasants outside France, impoverished by having to reimburse their former lords for their feudal and seigneurial rights, found themselves worse off than their counterparts in France, with less chance of becoming proprietors or of adding to their small holdings. They had to be content in most instances with only the abolition of serfdom and the disappearance, more or less, of the seigneurial system. An unfinished revolution to be sure, but a revolution, thanks to Napoleon.

CHAPTER 5

Reverses and Fall

*I*n two years' time it all fell apart, destroyed by the coalition of the English oligarchy, the absolutist monarchies on the Continent, the national sentiment of the oppressed peoples, the lassitude of French public opinion, and the treachery of leading profiteers of the empire. The system failed under the pressure of economic war, and military defeat delivered the final blow.

In 1810, Napoleon was forty. The most flattering portraits by the court painters did not hide that thickness of feature that made the emperor reflect the decadence of certain of his ancient Roman forbears. But if he was no longer the workaholic who did not know what a full night's sleep was, Napoleon was hardly a broken or exhausted man, as his endurance under the Russian winter and the retreat from Moscow would demonstrate. The superman who used to give all his time to the affairs of state spent the intermission of 1810–1811 with his young wife and infant son. His intellectual powers were fully intact, but less than ever now did he admit to being wrong about anything. Errors were invariably attributed to circumstances or to other people, never to his own miscalculations. Such stubbornness and self-infatuation would prove fatal to him.

1. Public Opinion: Disaffection and Opposition

Among the causes of Napoleon's downfall must be counted the growing indifference and alienation of public opinion, both within France and without.

"Minor literature is for me; great literature is against me," the emperor used to say, thinking of Madame de Staël and Chateaubriand. This was only partly true outside France. Abroad, he sometimes had in his corner writers and publicists of renown. Goethe and Hegel had been hostile to the Jacobin dictatorship but now hoped for a regeneration of Germany under the leadership of the princes friendly to Napoleon. They followed the imperial regime with interest. In French intellectual circles, the most talented and widely read authors—the liberals, de Staël and Benjamin Constant, and the legitimist (royalist) Chateaubriand—reproached Napoleon for the authoritarian evolution of his regime while maintaining their attachment to public liberties and to property. Though the emperor spared them neither vexations nor annoyances, he had the good sense not to make martyrs of them.

Beyond French borders, intellectual opposition was not only of the salon variety. It fed as much on wounded national pride as on hostility to imperial despotism. In the Confederation of the Rhine, even more especially in the university milieux of Heidelberg and Jena, romantic and nationalist conservatives such as the Schlegel brothers, Novalis, and Goerres denounced Napoleon as the oppressor

of the German nation and called on Germans to unite in
the fight against him. In Napoleonic Germany, the opposition fed as well on the writings of Gentz, who had taken
refuge in Vienna, of Fichte, whose *Speeches to the German
Nation* were given in Berlin in 1808, and of Arndt (see *The
Spirit of the Times*). That a liberal such as Madame de Staël
would intrigue with so fierce an opponent of the Revolution
as the conservative Gentz demonstrates how hatred of Napoleon could unite opposites.

Neither within the empire nor in the allied states did
Napoleon succeed in permanently holding on to the loyalty
of the upper classes. In France, although the old aristocracy
was flattered by his courtship, it stayed secretly legitimist.
Outside France, the traditional nobilities (notwithstanding
the defection of certain liberal aristocrats in Spain and the
Rhine Confederation) never forgave the emperor for taking
their privileges away from them. Was not one of Napoleon's
most outspoken adversaries Baron Stein, whose lands had
been annexed when the Holy Roman Empire was disman-
tled?

At first the French clergy had saluted Napoleon as the
restorer of the church, but in the vassal states the clergy
was more reserved; they persisted in seeing him as the har-
binger of the Revolution. Everywhere they deeply resented
the loss of the clerical tax (the *dîme*), of their lands, and, in
general, the consequences of the policy of secularization to
which even legitimate sovereigns had had eager recourse.
Nor did the quarrel between the emperor and the pope help
matters. In the French empire, a few recalcitrant bishops
were imprisoned, and seminarians were subjected to military service. After his imprisonment, Pius VII refused canonical investiture of bishops named by the emperor, thus

paralyzing the concordat. Napoleon replied by reviving Gallicanism. The Declaration of the Four Articles of 1682 now became the law of the empire. It provided for calling a national council of bishops to consider the question of whether metropolitans had the right, in the absence of paper accord, to invest newly names bishops after a six-month delay. Yet despite their docility in other matters, the French episcopate dug in its heels about breaking with Rome over investiture. Royalists, of course, were delighted with deteriorating church-state relations, but most practicing Catholics were not interested because daily services were not interrupted.

The attitude of the bourgeoisie is harder to ascertain. Certainly in France, Holland, northern Italy, and the Hanseatic cities, shippers and merchants did not forgive Napoleon for ruining maritime commerce. Industrialists were grateful enough to Napoleon for banning British goods, but they protested the scarcity and costliness of sugar and coffee. The average consumer, struck in virtually all his needs for food and clothing by the scarcity of everything from coffee to tobacco to cotton, accumulated a growing list of smoldering grievances against the regime. Finally, the bourgeoisie never forgave Napoleon for removing it from government. Equally out of weariness as out of deliberate calculation, in 1814 the bourgeoisie accepted a liberalized empire that promised the advantages of Bonapartism without the inconveniences.

In the empire and the vassal states, the same forms of popular opposition arose: contraband and desertion. The magnitude of the problem became clearer when, to celebrate Wagram, an amnesty was offered to draft dodgers—and 100,000 men applied! On the other hand, placing the phe-

nomenon in perspective, the figures for draft dodging and
desertion, though they increased in proportion to the need
for men, was no more than 10 percent in 1813. Despite high
taxes and conscription, the deeper truth is that the masses
were not much affected by the imperial despotism, except
during a serious food crisis. The cereal harvest of 1810 was
poor, and that of 1811 even worse. The price of bread rose
outrageously until the government had to establish a price
ceiling [le maximum], a drastic measure not taken since the
height of the Jacobin dictatorship in 1793. This crisis coincided with an industrial decline in the autumn of 1810.
Beggars and vagabonds spread insecurity in the countryside
and caused riots in the cities. A hunger riot in Caen on 2
March 1812 ended with eight death sentences, one of which
was passed on a woman. Calm returned only with the good
harvest of 1812.

The first armed popular outbursts in the annexed departments did not occur until 1813–1814, and then not everywhere. Often it was the customs officials who were the
first victims (as in Hamburg and Amsterdam). Yet on the
whole, in France at least (excepting the west and Provence),
despite conscription and heavy taxation, the little people,
from artisans to peasants, remained staunchly faithful to
l'Empereur to the end. Did the Hundred Days prove anything less? It was invariably with them that the Napoleonic
legend sounded its greatest echo. This was less so in the
new departments and in the vassal states, however (re-
member Spain), especially in those regions where the peasants were not liberated from the feudal regime. (Where they
were liberated, as in Germany, for example, they never
ceased considering Napoleon their benefactor.)

In certain vassal states, opposition to the Napoleonic grip raised permanent opposition from the majority of the population against the foreign occupier. Beginning in 1809, in Calabria and Apulia, guerrilla warfare arose, swelled by deserters and draft dodgers and organized by a secret, revolutionary, and xenophobic society: the Carbonaries. The Spanish uprising that began in 1808 permitted England to open an entire second front of warfare as well as to break open the economic blockade.

2. The Failure of the Economic War

By 1809 because of the continental war, England actually surmounted the first serious obstacles posed by the blockade. Napoleon saw that it was impossible for him to stanch the flow of contraband, that the French cotton industry was dying for want of raw material, and that French exports of agricultural products, and therefore French customs receipts, were falling off badly. He undertook a series of measures to remedy these problems. But he still viewed the countries of the Continent as so many colonies of his empire, forcing them to sell their raw materials to French industry and accord most-favored-nation status to French manufactured goods, even though their own manufactured goods were prohibited in France.

In the fight against contraband, Napoleon made one annexation after another of any and all territories where a black market in English trade prospered: Holland, the Hanseatic cities, Berg, several Rhenish states (even though one of them, the Duchy of Oldenburg, belonged to a relative of his ally the tsar), and finally Catalonia. At the same time, with the decree of Fontainebleau (10 October 1810), he enforced his blockade by setting up a special provost courts to supplement the ordinary customs tribunals in prosecuting violators. All seized goods were burned. Throughout the empire and allied states, the bonfires burned brightly.

As much to restrain consumption of colonial goods as to augment customs receipts, the importation of non-British foreign products (especially North American and Levantine cotton) was authorized, though at exhorbitant tariffs (for example, 600 francs for a hundredweight of sugar). To ensure a uniform price for such items in Europe (and avoid fraud), French diplomacy arranged that these tariffs be applied wherever French influence was felt. Napoleon's fellow sovereigns fell reluctantly into line, for obvious compelling economic reasons.

This regime of licensing, perfected with the decrees of Saint-Cloud (3 and 25 July 1810), matched the objectives of the blockade and the continental system. The licenses, granted only to French and United States shippers, and then only on payment of a very high additional tax, permitted some trade with England. But this exception ruined the economies of allied and neutral countries. Only products grown on French soil qualified for legal export (except for grains after June 1810, because of the poor harvest). In return, licensed vessels had to import colonial goods and cotton. Under no conditions could English manufactured products be imported.

In England these measures had severe effects. Exports fell 10 percent from 1809 and 1810, and 28.5 percent the following year. Yet although its European trade diminished by 17 percent to 24 percent, the flourishing black market kept it higher than it had been before the Berlin Decree. England's worst problems were inflicted by Napoleon's successful commerce with the United States. British production collapsed. In textiles alone, salaries fell 30 percent from 1810 to 1812. Workers took out their frustrations on machines, but the Luddism of these years proved to be ultimately more the work of rebels than revolutionaries. Finally, because the British had stockpiled cereals, bread was costly but available, and there was no revolution.

Although the empire's balance of payments stayed positive and customs receipts climbed, there were plenty of economic difficulties. First of all, contraband flourished, as inevitably it would, given the paucity of such indispensable commodities as sugar, coffee, and tobacco. Illegal goods were irresistible on the black market. Smugglers found buyers everywhere, not least among heads of state who sought to protect, as best they could, their country's shipping interests. Even French consular agents (such as Bourrienne at Hamburg), and, more especially French customs officials, were known to turn a blind eye to contraband. The network of clandestine shipping was incredibly complex: goods were endlessly supplied out of vast English warehouses on Mediterranean and Channel islands, or in coastal corners hidden to the emperor's customs agents. As Napoleon increasingly dominated the littoral and closed these down, they would merely move further east and reopen for business. Despite his best efforts, the city of Strasbourg held onto its title of contraband capital. Outside the empire, three major centers carried on a brisk business in contraband. Frankfurt, supplied via the North Sea, in its turn supplied Strasbourg and Basle. Leipzig, replenished via the Baltic and North seas, took care of Poland and Russia. And finally, Vienna took in contraband from Malta (via Trieste), Constantinople, and Salonika, and sold it throughout the Habsburg domains.

Presently, a severe if fleeting economic crisis shook the Continent. Although Napoleon was not responsible for the poor harvests, his policies and government nonetheless took the blame for the hammerblows that struck shipping, banking, and industry. Licensing had led to wide speculation in colonial commodities, whose prices climbed rapidly from April to October of 1810—along with the demand for discounts. In September, a leading firm in Lubeck failed, followed by a bank in Amsterdam and several Parisian and Frankfurt affiliates. Public panic followed. Banks called in their capital loans from industry, passing on the blow to the textiles industry and especially to cotton and silk manufacturers. As usual, the imperial regime fell back on capital levies on conquered countries and contracting for large public works, and the crisis was soon weathered. But the economy stagnated until 1815.

Because he had twice delivered telling blows to the British economy (in 1807–1808 and 1810–1812), Napoleon had reason to believe in the success of his blockade, *providing* that it was complete and it lasted. But such did not happen. Tsar Alexander, furious that the blockade worked solely to the French advantage, decided at the end of 1809 to tax French imports and to open his ports to neutral vessels. The Russian winter would effectively end the blockade and save England.

The fundamental reason that Napoleon lost the economic war was because, since Trafalgar, he could not place "the British isles in a state of seige." Mistress of the seas, England was able to open new markets for herself in Latin America and southern Europe, and thanks to her savvy diplomats and businessmen, she was able to avoid an extended hiatus in United States trade.

Napoleon was also a victim of errors in his economic policies. Convinced that Britain's financial armor was crumbling, he never thought to stanch the flow of currency and letters of exchange between England and the Continent. Instead, he respected the solidarity of international banking that leaped the Channel and closely linked Dutch and German firms with the Bank of England. Because English credit never stopped flowing to the Continent, the Continent sustained English shipping.

France found it impossible to play her traditional role of clearinghouse for raw colonial goods. When England tried, but failed, to replace her, consumer prices for perceived necessities, despite abundant contraband, stayed high all over Europe, as did the level of frustration and discontent.

French industry, moreover, was simply not able to meet the European demand for goods that used to be bought from the British. At best, French manufactured goods were available, but at a high price, thus favoring contraband. France increased production of metals, chemicals, and (despite the paucity of cotton) textiles, but it was not enough; she could not supplant Great Britain.

Nor could French markets absorb the equivalent amount of goods from her allies and neutral states that Great Britain had been able to do. This was particularly true with the naval supplies and cereals of the Baltic countries. France enjoyed abundant harvests most (if not all) years. What did she need with Baltic crops?

In sum, the reason for the failure of the economic war must be sought in the internal contradictions of Napoleon's policies. Asking heavy sacrifices of Europe, he offered nothing in return. Saddled with high tariffs, limited internal markets, and the politics of the blockade, the French empire was not a sufficient consumer nor a sufficient producer for her allies and for neutral states. Napoleon failed by seeing only the immediate interests of French industry. The blockade was killed by protectionism and by the economic ambitions of the continental system, that is, by French economic imperialism.

3. The Military Defeats

Napoleon's military defeats are explained by the weakening of his armies because of the rise in under-educated youthful conscripts, by employing foreign contingents of often dubious loyalty, by the paucity of good horses, and by the gradual decline in the quality of French arms. As the condition and position of his adversaries steadily improved, Napoleon's strategy lost its efficacy on the great plains of the east. Finally, it cannot be overlooked that the emperor was now compelled to fight on all fronts at once, and not just against armies but whole peoples in arms.

The operations against Russia did not commence until June of 1812, but even in 1810 and 1811, Napoleon's armies were far from being just soldiers on parade. In 1810, Marshal Masséna led 100,000 men on a pitiless mission to restore order in the Iberian peninsula. He was at first successful—opening the road all the way to Portugal—but in May 1811 Masséna was beaten by an Anglo-Portuguese army, and in consequence was cashiered by Napoleon. Early in 1812, Wellington arrived in Spain. On 22 July, he crushed Marmont and Clausel at Arapiles and drove King Joseph from Madrid. Napoleon was obliged to leave no fewer than 200,000 men in Spain at just the time he could have used them in the Russian invasion.

The Russian Disaster (1812)

The reasons for the breakdown of Franco-Russian relations were many. First, Napoleon was angry with the tsar both for his half-hearted support during the Austrian campaign and for refusing to give him the hand of a Russian princess. Alexander could not be reassured that the Grand Duchy of Warsaw was not intended as the core of a future kingdom of Poland, a serious threat to Russia. He was also good and sick of the blockade, not to mention discontented with Napoleon's high-handed annexation of the Duchy of Oldenburg, which had belonged to the tsar's brother-in-law.

The years 1811 and 1812 saw tensions between the two powers rise, while quietly each side sought to ensure that it had allies. The tsar managed to obtain Sweden's support by promising Norway to its regent, Count Bernadotte. He also signed a pact with Turkey. Napoleon forced Prussia to furnish 20,000 men, and Austria 30,000 (against the future return of the Illyrian provinces).

Counting all the allied troops, Napoleon assembled 1,100,000 men, of whom 200,000 were stationed in Spain and an equal number in Italy and France. The remaining 700,000 were concentrated in Germany and Poland, of whom 500,000 were on the front line. Only half of the latter came from the French Empire, and only about 125,000 to 140,000 were born within the boundaries of the old kingdom of France (the rest hailed from the new departments). The largest allied contingents were supplied by Holland, Germany, Poland, Switzerland, and even Spain. Twenty nations were represented in all. Except in the guard regiments, only one-tenth of the French units were tested veterans. The sheer size of the army obliged Napoleon to turn over large commands to Ney, Eugène de Beauharnais, and

Jerome Bonaparte, none of whom had experience with units of this magnitude and compactness. Finally, the display of luxury by numerous general and field officers goaded many rank-and-file soldiers to be undisciplined.

Napoleon set off on the campaign, his head stuffed with false expectations. First he thought that the Russian serfs would rise up the moment word reached them of the principles of 1789, principles that they had never heard speak of till then. Yet he never even issued an emancipation decree, fearing that it would compromise his expected reconciliation with the tsar, which of course did not happen. Then Napoleon anticipated that the ruble would fall. He even brought along masses of counterfeit to hurry that end. Finally, hoping that Alexander would come to terms before the winter, the French emperor decided not to burden his soldiers with heavy fur coats or ice shoes for the horses.

The immensity of the territory, the tenacity of the Russians, and the guerrilla war waged by the peasants swiftly quashed hopes of a brief campaign. Napoleon collided with a fierce national resistance supported by no less fierce national terrain and climate (though it is fair to say that the debacle had already begun before winter set in). To ensure tranquility at home, Napoleon had ordered his prisoner, Pope Pius VII, transferred to the palace of Fontainebleau (March 1812) for better surveillance.

On 24 June 1812, this motley army of twenty nations forded the Nieman. Inferior in number, the Russians retreated without giving pitched battle. No natural obstacle loomed where Napoleon could hem them in and force a showdown. Instead, the French exhausted themselves giving chase to an elusive enemy. Already by the middle of August, the French had lost 150,000 men to sickness and desertion. Horses were dying in such number in the heat that basic services ceased. The emperor would have had his men live off the land, but the army found only blackened earth at its approach, while encouraging marauding promoted desertion, particularly among the foreign troops. Napoleon tried in vain to envelop the Russians at Smolensk; his army, so much less homogeneous than in earlier days, lacked the rapid manoeuvrability he needed.

Before Moscow, the Russian commander, Marshal Kutuzov, finally offered battle. The butchery of Borodino and the Moskva (5–7 September) was worse than Eylau, but the Russian army, though defeated, was not destroyed and managed to retreat intact. Napoleon entered Moscow, but Alexander, pressed by his nobles and the German refugee "patriots" to stand fast, refused to negotiate. The city was ravaged by fires, depriving the French of badly needed supplies. With the Russian armies threatening his supply lines, the emperor ordered his 100,000 remaining troops to retreat.

Kutuzov drove them back onto the Smolensk road, devastated from the incoming march. Here they were harassed by Cossacks and peasant partisans who finished off the stragglers and wounded. On 5 November, the first winter offensive took place, lasting three days and losing 65,000 men. At the same time, Napoleon learned that in Paris the previous week, General Malet had barely failed to overthrow the regime by spreading the news that the emperor was dead. Curiously, in the panic that ensued, no one gave a thought to Napoleon II, the infant king of Rome. The weakness of the dynasty in public opinion was thus vividly revealed. After 14 November, the great cold of the Russian winter enveloped the French army, and the retreat became a debacle. Crossing the Beresina River (26–29 November), Napoleon's forces barely escaped annihiliation by the Russians. On 5 December, the emperor left the army for Paris. Not two weeks later, the tattered debris of his forces, 18,000 men, crossed back over the Niemen. The French had lost at least 380,000 men, including more than 100,000 prisoners, and 1,200 cannon.

In Spain, too, the year ended badly for France. Andalusia was irrevocably lost, with the English now disposing of solid operational bases for the coming campaign.

The Disasters of 1813

Napoleon immediately undertook to rebuild his army. By calling up 120,000 men from the "class" of 1813, including 100,000 who had been exempt for various reasons in the "classes" of 1805–1812, 180,000 national guard troops, and the soldiers recalled from Spain, he was able to scrounge up 350,000 men to try to hold Germany. But he was sorely lacking in officers and in cavalry, and his armaments were increasingly defective. At the battle of Katzbach, two-thirds of the rifles in certain regiments could not fire. The carriages and wheels of French cannon were made of uncured wood that broke under stress.

On 30 December 1813 and again on 30 January 1814, the news broke that Prussian and Austrian army corps, making up the north and south wings respectively of the French forces, defected. Napoleon fell back on the Oder and the Elbe. In February, the Russians occupied Poland. In the German campaign that now opened, Napoleon committed several serious errors, notably dispersing his troops too widely and expending too much time and forces defending such fortified cities as Danzig, Stettin, and Hamburg. Surprisingly, he seemed to have forgotten the most fundamental element of his doctrine of warfare: concentration of troops. Meanwhile, major popular uprisings broke out in the French rear, inhibiting the army's movements.

The first important insurrection took place even before the Austro-Prussian entry into the war against the French. In February 1813, the Hanseatic cities rose up with support from the Cossacks. Marshal Davout could barely contain the situation. On the 28th of that month, Prussia concluded an alliance with Russia, and a little more than two weeks later she entered the war against her former ally. Pushed hard by his own "patriots," the Prussian king appealed to the people of Germany to unite against the French yoke. A few days later, in response, the two Mecklemburg duchies and the four principalities of Anhalt seceded from the Confederation of the Rhine and placed their troops at the disposal of the allies.

In Holland, mutinies broke out among the soldiers, who demanded the return of the prince of Orange. On 17 March, Joseph left Madrid for good. Hoping to assuage Catholic opinion, Napoleon attempted a rapprochement with the pope. On 25 January he imposed the Concordat of Fontainebleau on Pius, but two months later the pope retracted his accord.

Napoleon took the offensive in Saxony in the spring of 1813, and, by a brilliant manoeuvre, beat the Prussians and the Russians at Lutzen (2 May) and Bautzen (21 May), but, with insufficient cavalry, could not destroy them. Austria offered to mediate and an armistice was signed at Pleiswitz (4 June).

Vienna thus became the arbiter. On 14 June, Prussia, Russia, and England concluded an agreement (the Reichenbach Convention) pledging not to make peace with France unless she reverted to her 1792 boundaries. Now, at the Congress of Prague, Metternich made Napoleon a better offer: that he return all French conquests except for the left bank of the Rhine and northern Italy. If the French rejected this proposal, Austria would rejoin the coalition. Napoleon refused to make any concessions just as he learned that Wellington had driven Marshal Soult back to the Basque border. The continental system thus ended as one by one European countries opened their ports to British goods. On 7 August, Austria threw down her ultimatum: return France to its 1800 borders or go to war. Napoleon picked the latter.

For the first time, Napoleon faced a coalition under a unified command. The Austrian general, Schwartzenberg, boasted 500,000 men, including the Swedes under Napoleon's former marshal, Bernadotte. The emperor could barely field half that number, and their training was inadequate. He beat the Austrians at Dresden (26 August) but the allies forced him and his marshals into a long series of marches and countermarches that exhausted his troops and encouraged desertion, especially among the German units. His lieutenants were beaten one after the other; thus, in two weeks Napoleon lost 150,000 men and nearly all his artillery.

On 30 September 1813, the Prussian Free Corps under Tchernischeff raided Cassel, signalling the collapse of the Kingdom of Westphalia and the flight of King Jerome. A fortnight later, the people of Bremen threw open their doors to the Russian troops of Tettenborn. The signal for the dissolution of the entire Confederation of the Rhine was given in none other than Bavaria, the state most favored by Napoleon. Munich joined the Austrians with a contingent of troops larger than any it had ever sent to the French.

To avoid encirclement, Napoleon fell back on Leipzig, where he was eventually compelled to fight (16–19 October). The arrival of Bernadotte's 100,000 Swedes at the height of the battle, the defection of the Saxon contingents, lack of artillery everywhere, and the passivity of certain Napoleonic commanders, such as Augereau, explained the defeat—a defeat that cost the French 60,000 men. What remained of their army fell back on the Rhine, flattening the Austro-Bavarian force at Hanau when they attempted to block its route. All of Germany now joined the victors. In November, the French withdrew to their side of the Rhine. But, hoping to retake Germany, Napoleon had left 100,000 men and 1,000 cannon in forts along the Vistula, the Oder,and the Elbe. They held on until 1814, but dispersed between Basle and Nimegen there were no more than 56,000 French troops to resist 230,000 allies.

On the other fronts, the situation was equally disastrous. Ten days before Leipzig, Wellington crossed the Bidassoa, forcing Napoleon to return the Spanish throne to Ferdinand VII. In November, Austria invaded Italy and was reinforced by English troops landing in Tuscany. Prince Eugène fought the allies every foot of the way, but in Naples Marshal Murat negotiated with the British and eventually opened his ports to them. In November, Holland fell, and the next month, Switzerland denounced the Act of Mediation and opened her country to the allies. Russian troops were stationed in Amsterdam, where the prince of Orange reclaimed his states. Gravest of all, on 23 December Austrian troops appeared in Alsace.

The Campaign of France and the
First Abdication (1814)

As early as 9 November the allies offered peace if France would revert to her 1792 borders. Napoleon decided to accept, for French opinion yearned for peace and in Paris a conspiracy threatened a regency under Joseph or Count Bernadotte. But when the emperor communicated his acceptance of their terms, the allies replied that it was too late. On the home front, the Legislative Body in Paris demanded in December the guarantee of civil and political freedoms and invited the emperor not to make war any more "except to ensure the independence and security of [French] territory. In effect, it condemned all of Napoleon's policies. For this, the Legislative Body was dissolved, but in the west of France, royalism again reared its head.

On 9 October, the government had called for 120,000 men of the 1814 "class," and again as many from the "class" of 1815. A month later, it called up another 300,000. But the French nation balked before such sacrifices. National opinion wanted peace at nearly any price. There was frankly no strong reaction against invasion, or against the Russo-Prussian cruelties, except in the occupied areas. The emperor thus did not dare replay the 1793 scenario by calling for the *levée en masse*. Under the circumstances, when military operations recommenced, he could field only 70,000 poorly equipped men on the northeast front, to confront 260,000 coalition troops.

As the allies swept through Montbéliard, Dole, Dijon, and Langres (January 1814), Napoleon paid dearly for neglecting to strengthen the frontier fortresses of the Old Regime. The Prussian general, Blücher, and his Austrian counterpart, Schwartzenberg, easily got as far as Champagne because no proper fortifications had been readied to resist them. By then it was too late to prepare much of a defense. Leaving to Soult the task of stemming Wellington's advance in Aquitaine, and to Eugène the task of holding Italy (against, among others, the forces of Murat, who had betrayed his emperor in a vain attempt to hold on to his throne at Naples), Napoleon devoted himself to the northeastern front. Before leaving to take command, he ordered the pope to be taken back to Rome.

Bülow and his Anglo-Prussians descended into the valley of the Oise, while Blücher, with the main Prussian army, stayed by the Marne, and Schwartzenberg with his Austrians and Russians, took the Aube. At last finding himself again in a theater of operations that favored his tactical principles, Napoleon manoeuvred skillfully among the enemy armies. While in the North, the French general, Maison, with his back to the fortresses of Vauban, held in check the Russians under Wintzingerode, Napoleon was able to move rapidly between the Aube and the Marne. The emperor took the Prussians by surprise and scattered them at Champaubert and Montmirail (10 and 14 February), then broke up the Austrians at Montereau (18 February).

Discouraged, the allies were about to accept the peace that Napoleon offered, which agreed to the earlier Frankfurt proposal (France's 1800 boundaries). But shamed and toughened by the English diplomat, Castlereagh, who would not hear of any terms except the 1792 frontiers, they finally stood firm. By March, the situation was worsening for France. On the 16th, Augereau, entrusted with the defense of the Jura, was beaten, and soon afterward abandoned Lyon to the Austrians without a fight. Soult fell back on Toulouse, and on the 14th, Wellington took Bordeaux where the royalist mayor and the duke d'Angoulême proclaimed the restoration of the Bourbon dynasty. Meanwhile Bernadotte was marching steadily along the Oise with 100,000 men.

Numbers carried the day. After negotiations broke off (19 March), Napoleon attempted to destroy Blücher by the Aisne. Trying to buy time, the Prussian field marshal laid siege to the fortified city of Soissons, which capitulated and gave Blücher the protection he needed, for Napoleon had not the time to lay siege in turn. Unable to stop the allies at Laon, the emperor gave up hope of preventing their march on Paris. He thought instead to go to Lorraine, where the population had risen up against the invaders, raise another army and strike the allies in their rear. But his plans were foiled.

Invited in by the royalists, the allies took Paris, a city without fortifications which nonetheless defended itself valliantly (18,000 casualties on each side). On 3 April, the Senate, carefully prepared by Talleyrand, voted to oust Napoleon. At the same time, the emperor arrived at Fontainebleau, where he was acclaimed by the army. On hearing news of the senatorial vote, he wanted to march forthwith on Paris. But his marshals, unlike their troops, refused to collaborate and instead forced Napoleon to abdicate in favor of his son. Lefebvre summed up his colleagues's attitudes thus, "Did [Napoleon] imagine that after he had endowed us with lands, titles, and income that we would then get ourselves killed for him? It's his own fault: he made life too easy for us." Heaping treachery on cowardice, one of Napoleon's generals, Marmont, led his troops over to the allies (4–5 April), taking with him any prayer that his former emperor had of recommencing the fight. The allies now imposed unconditional abdication on Napoleon (6 April), and the very same day, the Senate—which still contained more than a handful of regicides from the Revolutionary Convention—actually voted to recall Louis XVIII to the throne of his ancestors. On the 20th of the month, Napoleon said a sad farewell to his guard at Fontainebleau, the only regiment to remain steadfast to the last, and left for Elba.

Earlier, on the 10th, Soult gave final (and losing) battle to Wellington outside the walls of Toulouse. Little less than a month later, Davout capitulated at Hamburg. It was the end.

From the Island of Elba to Saint Helena

The allies permitted Napoleon to keep the title of emperor and accorded him full sovereignty of the island of Elba, together with an annual income of 2 million francs (104 million today [$1,750,000]), to be paid by the French government. En route to his new state, Napoleon traveled down the valley of the Rhone, where he learned just how unpopular he had become. In early May he reached Portoferraio and immediately set out in a whirl of activity to reorganize the administration of his new state. But cares and boredom appeared quickly enough. His wife and son did not join him; the annual stipend was not paid, and it was reported that in Vienna the allies were mulling over the idea of exiling him further—to the island of Saint Helena. Napoleon was well aware that in France certain of his former loyalists were conspiring to bring him back, just as he was well aware of the profound discontent that the new government was inspiring among the people, among the bourgeois purchasers of the nationalized lands, and in the army. After slipping away from Elba on 25 February 1815, he landed in France at the Golfe-Juan on 1 March.

What Chateaubriand once called "the invasion of a country by one man" turned out to be a catastrophe for France. The mayor of a village well limned the situation when he said to Napoleon, "We had just started to become happy and peaceful again when you returned to cause trouble." Avoiding the royalist Rhone valley this time, the emperor traveled to Paris via the Alps. Everywhere he spoke the revolutionary language of 1793, posing as the defender of land purchasers, hostile to the re-establishment of the medieval ecclesiastical tax and of feudal rights and privileges. Striking at the nobility, he promised "to string them up to the lanterns." Not surprisingly, therefore, the common man won over the foot soldier and the foot soldier won over his officers (for example, Ney, at Auxerre) to the emperor's cause. On 20 March, Napoleon once again set foot in the Tuileries in Paris. Louis XVIII had gone into exile during the previous night.

Those bourgeois notables who reacted with fright at this recrudescence of Jacobinism should have saved themselves from getting excited, for Napoleon never had the slightest intention of basing his rule on the people. But he did realize that he could not simply re-establish the imperial regime as it had become by 1814. So he promulgated the Additional Act to the Constitutions of the Empire, a document he drew up himself, working with the liberal thinker Benjamin Constant. The Additional Act was a bastard compromise which satisfied no one, not the notables, for it provided for universal suffrage, nor the people, for it re-established the imperial peerage.

The ratification plebiscite was thus a defeat: 1,300,000 yes votes, 4,000 noes, but 4,700,000 abstentions. Royalist uprisings exploded up and down the Rhone Valley as well as in Bordeaux and Toulon. The Vendée and Brittany broke into actual insurrection: Napoleon had to send in an army of 20,000 men—men he would sorely need at Waterloo.

Naturally, Napoleon's fate would be determined by arms. For the sake of appearances, and because French public opinion was weary of war, the emperor bent over backwards to issue peaceful proclamations to the allies, but they were not deceived. Virtually all Europe took the field against Napoleon—a million men in arms. War was inevitable.

The emperor nonetheless refused to decree the national levy [the *levée en masse*]. Obliged to disperse 100,000 men in the Vendée and along the frontiers of the Pyrénées, the Var, the Alps, and the Jura, he managed to collect a fine army of 125,000 men to march to Belgium. This time, Napoleon was able to count on a high percentage of old veterans, high-quality artillery, and enough cavalry, but dependable lieutenants were lacking. Many of his marshals had of course gone over to the enemy, but some were frankly exhausted. The excellent Davout having been named minister of war, Napoleon was forced to entrust to Marshal Ney the task of overseeing the army's complicated manoeuvres—and Ney was no manoeuverer.

Marching directly to Belgium, the emperor intended to take on separately the armies of Wellington and Blücher. At Ligny on 16 June he beat back Blücher but could not destroy him. Leaving Marshal Grouchy to finish off the Prussians, Napoleon marched against Wellington. The latter, entrenched on the plateau of Mont-Saint-Jean before Waterloo, defended himself well with precise use of artillery. Poorly directed by Ney, the French frontal attack failed to destroy the English squares. The unexpected arrival of Prussian forces under Bülow on the right flank, followed by Blücher (who had outwitted Grouchy), inundated the French. It was a rout.

Aware of Napoleon's tenacious popularity with the people of Paris, Carnot, Davout, and Napoleon's brother Lucien now begged the emperor to proclaim the revolutionary levée en masse to bring the nation to arms. On the other hand, the legislative chambers were intractable in their opposition, and so Napoleon was forced again to abdicate (22 June).

This time, meeting cheers en route, he arrived at the port of Rochefort where he surrendered to the English. He was deported to the island of Saint Helena, where he died on 5 May 1821, after five years, six months, and twenty-seven days of captivity—a period that earned him as much glory as the victory at Austerlitz.

Conclusion

"In life he missed having the whole world; in death, he had it. After suffering the despotism of his person, we are now subjected to the despotism of his memory." Better than any others, these words of Chateaubriand capture the post-Napoleonic era. Napoleon's system of warfare profoundly marked military thought. The German general Von Schlieffen claimed he had spent hours meditating on Napoleon's manoeuvres at Ulm before drawing up his famous plan. Elaborating his doctrine for using tanks, another famous German officer, Güderian, admitted he had carefully studied Napoleon's pursuit of the enemy after Jena.

As for the grand balance after the Napoleonic wars, it is heavy with consequences. For one thing, the wars were responsible for the dimunition of France's weight in Europe. The country had lost over a million men (half of them were missing). Coupled with the relentless drop in the French birth rate throughout the nineteenth century, the bloodletting of the Napoleonic wars largely accounts for the decline of French power after 1815. Never again would France by herself be able to win a war in Europe.

The allies would take vengeance on France for the troubles they had reaped during the Revolution and the empire.

Whether the regime was legitimist, Orleanist, republican, or Bonapartist, the French state would for decades be held in suspicion by her neighbors. A *cordon sanitaire* went up around French frontiers: the Lower Countries protected Anvers for Great Britain, the Swiss Confederation was neutralized. The breaches opened on France's north and northeastern frontiers became sites for invasion in 1870 and in the twentieth century. The French took the second treaty of Paris (1815) as a humiliation; indeed, their resentment came to embrace the whole accord signed by the allies at the Congress of Vienna. The psychology of this resentment would largely explain the foreign policy of Napoleon III (1848–1870). Spain, even more than Napoleon, was the great loser in the war that was fought on its soil. She suffered hundreds of thousands of casualties; much of her national wealth was destroyed, and her American colonies wavered on the edge of secession. Perhaps worst of all, Spain's enlightened elites—those social elements that might have brought their country to participate in the great innovations of European history of that era—had become too intimately associated with the French occupiers. They lost much of their courage and will, along with their respect in the nation's mind.

Following the war of American independence and the revolution of 1789, the Napoleonic wars sounded the death knell of European domination of the American continent. After this, the colonial powers turned to Africa and Asia.

Napoleon's hegemony in Europe also delivered decisive strokes to the Old Regime, even if it did not cause its immediate and complete disappearance. Only thus can one understand why a German and socialist philosopher such as Engels would regret that French hegemony had not lasted longer in Germany. The people who bought nationalized church lands would do their best to pull agriculture out of its lethargy. In industry, abolishing corporatist constraints and creating a permanent system of free enterprise promoted capitalism.

The economic war that Napoleon carried on with the blockade and the continental system also left deep traces. The interruption of maritime commerce caused a definitive decline in certain old industries that had depended upon overseas markets: the Westphalian linen industry, for example. On the other hand, industries that competed with British production were strengthened. The birth of a Europe-based cotton industry in Switzerland, Alsace, and Saxony owes little to Napoleon personally, but owes much to the temporary end of trade with England. Industry was not able to develop in Spain and Italy because these were areas held almost as market-fiefs by French producers; thus industrialization (and development) came late to these countries. Contraband was responsible for the first appearance of that now familiar phenomenon, the overnight millionaire, in such cities as Strasbourg, Frankfurt, and Cologne. The wars also encouraged the accumulation of large amounts of capital, which after 1815 would be invested in industry and banking. Thanks to the blockade, Frankfurt, the turnstyle of the blackmarket, developed its financial services. The era saw the debut of the Rothschild fortune, not only in Frankfurt, but also in London and Paris. This sort of empire held firm when Napoleon's shook to its roots.

In other words, Napoleon's political policies established deep and important economic infrastructures. Because of the temporary paralysis in maritime communications, intercontinental communication took on greater importance. Roads and rivers replaced the sea. Was it not the emperor himself who confided to Las Cases on Saint Helena, "Do you want to know what are my real treasures? They are the Antwerp basin, the maritime works of Venice, the beautiful roads from Antwerp to Amsterdam, from Mainz to Metz and from Bordeaux to Bayonne, the Simplon, Mont-Cenis, and Montgenèvre [Alpine] passes, or the Corniche pass, which opens the Alps in four directions." He might well have added the roads of the Illyrian provinces, which for many years, until the coming of railroads, "reminded everyone of Napoleon's customs agents and the brief dominion of his continental system." It would be Wilhemine Germany that finally realized a project voted by the French Senate in 1810: the junction of the Baltic and North seas by a canal connecting Lubeck to Hamburg (later elongated to reach the Rhine).

If the Revolution had taught the French that any weakening of the executive power condemned the state to impotence and brought the country to anarchy, the Napoleonic experience showed them that *any* authority could lead to despotism. After 1815 they forever dreamed of a regime that could conciliate order and freedom, and it is perhaps because this equilibrium is always difficult to maintain that Bonapartism was not extinguished in the courtyard at Fontainebleau where Napoleon said adieu to the guard. Rather, it has resurged each time that the French, wearied of the impotent infighting of political parties, feel the need to be governed, each time that the political elites find themselves incapable of surmounting the problems they have created for the country. It was in such circumstances that power was handed to Louis-Napoleon in 1848, to Clemenceau in 1917, to Pétain in 1940, and to DeGaulle in 1958—

always with the afterthought that the savior could be got rid of the moment he was not needed.

The consulate and the empire deeded to France the administrative and juridical framework which she has kept almost intact to this day. The recent creation of a system of decentralization has not altered the country's devotion to that Napoleonic principle that holds that localities are best governed by a mix of locally elected representatives and centrally appointed officials. (Nonetheless, under Mitterrand, the power of the former has been increased at the expense of the latter.) The permanence of the great institutions withstanding all political instability, erected by Napoleon—the magistracy, the Council of State, the Bank of France, the *Cour des Comptes*, and the major departments of government—has ensured continuity for the country. It is from Napoleon's time—not before, not after—that the high school diploma [the *baccalauréat*] attained the prestige and popularity that it has never lost. And has anyone ever refused the Legion of Honor on the grounds that it originated during the empire? The Civil Code, despite adjustment for time and place, remains the foundation of private law for nearly 300 million people in the Old and New Worlds.

Through legend Napoleon entered history a second time. On Saint Helena he carefully crafted the image that he wished posterity to hold of him: defender of the oppressed nationalities, champion of peace forced into war by the powers of the Old Regime, rampart of liberties become despot only reluctantly and by necessity. Even more than his book, *Mémorial de Sainte-Hélène*, the troubadours whose songs created the real Napoleonic legend were his former soldiers—men who somehow forgot the suffering they had undergone and thought rather of the glory and the excitement they experienced in their forced marches throughout Europe. Trying to turn the legend to advantage for his own regime, King Louis Philippe ordered the return of the emperor's remains in 1840—only a short time after the *second* failed coup d'etat against the king's government by Napoleon's nephew, Louis-Napoleon.

With time, Napoleon passed imperceptibly from legend into myth, for the life and misfortunes of vanquished heroes never cease being the stuff of imagination. For literature, the theater, the music hall, even for the detective novel, the legend of Napoleon is an inexhaustible mine. Thus has he installed himself permanently not only in the French, but virtually in the human, collective memory. In 1940, hoping to ingratiate himself at least a little with the French, Adolf Hitler thought it wise to send back to France the remains of Napoleon's son, "l'Aiglon" (the young eagle). In 1969, for the bicentenary of Napoleon's birth, postage stamps were issued with Napoleon's effigy—in the Arab Emirates! Thus breaking out of the domain reserved to professional historians, Napoleon will forever confirm his own place in human history. And this is all no less true because the French embassy in Lagos, in an excess of republican zeal, saw fit in 1985 to distribute a pamphlet entitled *Two Thousand Years of the History of France* that does not once mention the name of Napoleon Bonaparte. Instead, the pamphlet neatly sums up the years 1804–1815 as "Monarchy Restored."

Selected Bibliography

Bergeron, Louis. *France Under Napoleon*. Princeton: Princeton University Press, 1981, orig. pub., 1972.

Bruun, Geoffrey. *Europe and the French Imperium, 1799–1814*. Westport, Ct.: Greenwood Press, 1983, orig. pub., 1938.

Castelot, Andre. *Napoleon*. New York: Harper & Row, 1971.

Chandler, David G. *The Campaigns of Napoleon*. New York: Macmillan, 1966.

———. *Dictionary of the Napoleonic Wars*. New York: Macmillan, 1979.

———. *Napoleon's Marshals*. New York: Macmillan, 1986.

Connelly, Owen. *Blundering to Glory: Napoleon's Military Campaigns*. Wilmington, Del.: Scholarly Resources, 1987.

———. *Napoleon's Satellite Kingdoms*. New York: The Free Press, 1965.

———. *French Revolution: Napoleonic Era*. New York: Holt, Rinehart & Winston, 1979.

Cronin, Vincent. *Napoleon*. New York: Morrow, 1972.

Ellis, Geoffrey. *Napoleon's Continental Blockade: The Case of Alsace*. New York: Oxford University Press, 1981.

Elting, John. *Swords Around the Throne, Napoleon's "Grande Armée."* New York: The Free Press, 1988.

Gieyl, Pieter. *Napoleon: For and Against*. New Haven: Yale University Press, 1949.

———, ed. *The Mind of Napoleon, A Selection from His Written and Spoken Words*. New York: Columbia University Press, 1955.

Herold, J. Christopher. *Bonaparte in Egypt*. New York: Harper & Row, 1962.

Holtman, Robert. *The Napoleonic Revolution*. Baton Rouge: Louisiana State University Press, 1979, orig. pub., 1967.

Horne, Alistair. *Napoleon, Master of Europe, 1805–1807*. London: Weidenfeld & Nicolson, 1979.

Kafker, Frank, and James M. Laux, eds. *Napoleon and His Times: Selected Interpretations*. Malaber, Fl.: Krieger, 1989.

Kennedy, Emmet. *Destutt de Tracy and the Origins of "Ideology."* Philadelphia: American Philosophical Society, 1978.

Lefebvre, Georges. *Napoleon*. 2 vols. New York: Columbia University Press, 1969, orig. pub., 1935.

Ludwig, Emil. *Napoleon*. New York: Boni & Liveright, 1926.

Tulard, Jean. *Napoleon: The Myth of the Saviour*. London: Weidenfeld and Nicolson, 1984, orig. pub., 1977.

MacKenzie, Norman. *The Escape from Elba, The Fall and Flight of Napoleon, 1814–1815*. New York: Oxford University Press, 1982.

Markham, Felix. *Napoleon*. New York: New American Library, 1964.

Meyer, Jack Allen. *An Annotated Bibliography of the Napoleonic Era, Recent Publications, 1945–1985*. Westport, Ct.: Greenwood Press, 1987.

Nicolson, Nigel. *Napoleon, 1812*. New York: Harper & Row, 1985.

O'Dwyer, Margarte. *The Papacy in the Age of Napoleon and the Restoration: Pius VII, 1800–1823*. Lanham, Md.: University Press of America, 1985.

Rothenberg, Gunther. *The Art of Warfare in the Age of Napoleon*. Bloomington, Ind.: Indiana University Press, 1980.

Whitcomb, Edward. *Napoleon's Diplomatic Service*. Durham, N.C.: Duke University Press, 1979.